So You Can't Stand Evangelism?

So You
Can't Stand
EVANGELISM?

A Thinking Person's Guide
to Church Growth

James R. Adams

COWLEY PUBLICATIONS
Cambridge ✦ Boston
Massachusetts

Published in the United States of America by Cowley Publications, a division of the Society of St. John the Evangelist. No portion of this book may be reproduced, stored in or introduced into a retrieval system, or transmitted, in any form or by any means—including photocopying—without the prior written permission of Cowley Publications, except in the case of brief quotations embodied in critical articles and reviews.

Library of Congress Cataloging-in-Publication Data:
Adams, James R., 1934-
    So you can't stand evangelism? : a thinking person's guide to church growth / James R. Adams.
        p.   cm.
    Includes bibliographical references.
    ISBN 1-56101-096-0 (alk. paper)
    1. Evangelistic work. 2. Church management. 3. Belief and doubt. 4. Non church-affiliated people—Religious life. 5. St. Mark's Church (Washington, D.C.: Episcopal). I. Title.
BV3790.A33   1994
269'.2—dc20   94-21573

This book is printed on recycled, acid-free paper and was produced in the United States of America.

Scripture quotations are taken from the *New Revised Standard Version* of the Bible.

Cowley Publications
28 Temple Place
Boston, Massachusetts 02111

for
Lesley, Gretchen, and Nancy

Table of Contents

Preface xi

Introduction 1

Part One

Chapter 1: The Limits of Conventional Evangelism 11
Resistance to Evangelism Within the Church
Evangelism and Institutional Survival
Evangelism Redefined

Chapter 2: A Feast for All Peoples 25
The Great Commission
Varieties of Skepticism
Standards for Membership

Chapter 3: The Promise of an Open Approach 38
Practical Advantages to Church Growth
Welcoming People with Doubts
Challenge and Stimulation
Hope for the Future

Chapter 4: The Costs of Evangelism 55
Identifying Fears
Careful Use of Religious Language
Surrendering Faith and Beliefs
Evangelism and Bible Study
The Problem of Reductionism

Part Two

Chapter 5: Adjusting the Message for
the Sake of the Mission 75
Adapting Christianity to Different Cultures
Adapting Christianity to Popular Ways of Thinking
Adapting Christianty to the Philosophy of Acquisition
Adapting Church Organization to Changing Conditions

Chapter 6: Offering a Gospel of Freedom
and Responsibility.. 92
    The Burdens of Shame and Guilt
    The Oppression of Fate
    The Chaos of Emptiness
Chapter 7: What Can We Say About Jesus? 110
    Jesus and His Friends of Little Faith
    Jesus as Teacher
    The Skepticism of Jesus
    Jesus as the Son of God

Part Three
Chapter 8: Creating a Climate for Growth....................... 127
    Permission to Argue
    Interactive Preaching
    Honest Inquiry
    Community Outreach
    Straight Talk About Money
    The Church and the Arts
    Baptisms, Weddings, and Funerals
Chapter 9: Planning for Action 147
    A Committee on Inclusion
    The Details of Parish Life
    The Congregation's Identity
    Equipping the Evangelists: Adult Education
    Preparation for Joining and Belonging
    Marketing the Gospel to the Skeptical
Chapter 10: Ongoing Evangelism.. 170
    How It Will Look
    Shared Authority and Responsibility
    Evangelism and Parish Dynamics
    Disenchantment and Maturity
    A Spirit of Generosity

Notes.. 189

Preface

Although I must assume full responsibility for the way I state the case for evangelism, this book represents the thinking and practice of a community, St. Mark's Church on Capitol Hill in Washington, D.C. Over the past twenty-eight years that I have served them as rector, the members of the congregation have taught me, challenged me, rebuked me, and supported me as I have tried to make the church more open to people with doubts and questions. While countless numbers of them contributed indirectly to the writing of this book, some of them had a direct hand in its production by providing me with the benefit of their critiques.

For most of my years at St. Mark's, I have had the benefit of a personal advisory committee that has provided me with wise counsel and that has periodically evaluated my work. This year the Rector's Advisory Committee took on an additional assignment, reading the rough drafts of these chapters as I produced them and sending me their comments. I am particularly grateful to three of them who wrote down the comments of the group and sent me copies of their notes—Jennifer Markley, Chris Wemple, and the convener, Susan Goodwillie—but my gratitude extends to all the other members of the group who took time to work over the material and offer their assessments: Peter Powers, Wende McIlwain, Martha Connor-Donnelly, Joanna Etka, Don Thibeau, and Louis Bayard.

I also received valuable guidance from three former church wardens, whose experience in governing the parish gave them a particularly useful perspective: Crane Miller, David Meade, and Janice Gregory. In addition, I had the advice of two other people who read what I was producing from their particular perspectives: Tom Getman, our resident conservative Christian, and Glen Hoptman, a practicing Jew whose rabbinical training has given him a sharp eye for evaluating Christianity.

Much as I appreciate the people who helped with the writing of the book, I would be remiss if I did not thank the vestry of St.

Mark's for providing me with a six-month sabbatical leave every seventh year. This book would not have been possible without uninterrupted time for reflection and writing. They also deserve my thanks for equipping me with a notebook computer and making it possible for me to rely on the services of two competent secretaries, Betty Smith and Mildred Wheat, who were responsible for getting copies of the drafts out to the readers. I am also grateful to Betty and Mildred for keeping the office going so well in my absence.

Finally, a word of thanks for Cowley Publications editor Cynthia Shattuck. I feel fortunate to have had the benefit of her wisdom. Often when I am reading a good book, I think to myself how much better a book it would have been if only Cynthia could have taken her red pen to the manuscript before it was published.

Jim Adams
Washington, D.C.

Introduction

In writing this book, I am trying to persuade church people that in their efforts at evangelism they should be more accepting of those who question Christianity—the doubters, skeptics, and agnostics among us. Instead of dismissing or attempting to convert those who cannot accept religious doctrine at face value, Christians might be more faithful to the cause of evangelism if they welcomed them into their ranks. I realize that the very word "evangelism" evokes certain fears among those of other religious persuasions and even among Christians themselves. In writing this book, I have tried to present evangelism in a way that will help Christians appreciate what they have to offer but will not threaten the integrity of other religious groups. Thoughtful evangelism can help Christians come to terms with their need for ritual and community and to understand how other people deal with those same needs. This approach promotes education, not conversion; it emphasizes serving over proselytizing.

I think St. Paul had the right approach to evangelism. He did not condemn Jews for being Jewish or Greeks for being gentiles. He did not try to get Jews to abandon Judaism or Greeks to repudiate their Hellenistic culture in order to follow Jesus of Nazareth. Following St. Paul's example, Christians today could responsibly welcome agnostic, doubting, and questioning people just as they are. Some people cannot help questioning. Perhaps they were born that way; perhaps their parents unwittingly goaded them into the habit when they were still quite young. How questioning people got that way, however, does not matter very much. The point is that some people cannot help pondering, wondering, and analyzing, which can make it difficult for them to accept statements of faith as statements of fact or miracles as historic events.

Of course everybody asks questions, but some people put much more emphasis on what they feel or believe than on what they think. Questioning people are not necessarily wiser or smarter than those who trust their feelings or stand by their beliefs, but they cannot help noticing disconnections and contradictions. For example, at Christmastime a questioning person who happens to attend worship services will notice that, contrary to what appears on Christmas cards, the familiar story in Luke does not mention a star over Bethlehem or a stable filled with animals. If sufficiently curious, such a person will find out that the star appears only in Matthew's gospel and that nowhere in the Bible is it written that animals witnessed the birth of Jesus. Other people do not seem to notice the difference between what the story says and what they have been led to believe, or if they do notice, they do not seem to care about the discontinuity between the gospel and tradition.

This need to understand often appears in early childhood. I can remember a time when I was just old enough to be out after dark in the summer. I was lying on my back in the prickly grass, scrutinizing the stars that decorated the vast Nebraska sky, and I could not help wondering: What lies beyond the stars? Does the universe have an end? If so, what is beyond the end? Such questions never failed to fill me with a sensation similar to what I experienced the first time I came up over the top and began the descent in a Ferris wheel at the county fair.

As an adult, I can still get that same agreeable feeling of terror in the pit of my stomach when I read in the newspaper about the latest discoveries in astronomy. One article reported that astronomers using the earth-orbiting Hubble space telescope had discovered in a spot of sky no bigger than one quarter of the moon's diameter seventy-three galaxies that are four billion light years away from the earth. The astronomers estimated that each of these seventy-three galaxies contains perhaps 200 billion stars. The realization that the light from these 14.6 trillion stars began the voyage to earth four billion years ago staggers the imagination. When I think about the vast extent of the universe, my mind starts to reel, but I cannot help pondering the new information.

Such pondering led me to a basic religious question: How could the creator of this vast universe have chosen only one method of self-revelation, a first-century craftsman-turned-teacher, Jesus of Nazareth?

As a questioning person, I have never been able to convince myself that Jesus of Nazareth offers the only way to God. Even as a youngster, I was offended by the words attributed to Jesus in the fourteenth chapter of John's gospel: "I am the way, and the truth, and the life. No one comes to the Father except through me." As an adult, I have come to understand that those words may represent a statement of personal faith made by the author or editor of the gospel rather than a claim made by Jesus himself, but for many years the use preachers made of this saying stood between me and the church.

That was not my only problem with religion. From an early age I could not help thinking about death, and I remember vividly the first time I realized that my life would not go on indefinitely. I was asleep in bed and then woke up, suddenly overwhelmed with terror. My breathing was labored and my heart was beating wildly. Someday I was going to die! I would not exist anymore. The world would go on without me. I leapt out of bed—lying under the covers was too much like being in a coffin. I went over to the window and sat there staring out at the night sky for a long time, until my heart calmed down and my breathing returned to normal. I told myself that if only I could believe what they taught me in Sunday school about God and going to heaven, I would not be afraid to die, but I knew in my heart that I did not believe a word of it.

During my high school and college years, several times I awoke suddenly in the middle of the night terrified by thoughts of death. Occasionally I tried to pray, but once I had taken up smoking, I found that a cigarette had a more calming effect than prayer. Try as I might, I simply could not believe that death was nothing more than passing on to a better life. Because heaven and God were so closely related in my mind, I was also unable to develop any faith in God. I wanted to believe; I simply couldn't.

When I was a senior in college, I began dating a young woman who invited me to attend church with her on Sunday morning. Afterward we could go out for breakfast and then get a paper and read the news and the comics together. I found the invitation appealing, especially the part about breakfast and the comics. At that point in my life, I had not been to church for seven or eight years, but I thought that I could put up with an hour or so of religion in exchange for the pleasure of her company for most of Sunday. What struck me as odd about the experience, once I had tried it, was that I did not object to the worship as much as I thought I would. In fact, over the winter months I became quite attached to what became our Sunday morning routine—so attached that when we eventually parted company, I continued with my new habit of going to church each Sunday. I found some sort of reassurance in the routine, but I still did not believe what I thought Christians were supposed to believe, and I was still subject to terrors of death in the night.

One Sunday morning, sitting in church by myself, I thought of a solution to my problem. If going to church was not enough to produce faith, then I should go the whole way to get religion—go to seminary and become an ordained minister. At that time, 1955, the churches were experiencing a serious shortage of clergy for their booming congregations. With no difficulty, I found a parish church that would sponsor me and a bishop who would accept me. Nobody asked me what I believed, so I soon found myself deeply engrossed in theological studies and on the track to ordination. By the time I completed my degree in theology three years later, I had convinced myself that I believed what I was supposed to believe.

After ordination I was put to work as an assistant minister with special responsibility for young adults. I organized groups to discuss the most profound questions facing human beings, such as "Who am I?" and "Who is God?"; at the end of each discussion I handed out the correct answers I had prepared in advance. As I recall, the "correct" response to the first was "I can find the answer only in Christ" and to the second, "We can conceive of God's nature having a threefold differentiation while existing as absolute unity." Looking back, I can hardly believe my arrogance in thinking I had the right answers to some of life's most baffling puzzles.

All went well until the senior minister of the church suggested that I might learn something useful about recent innovations in adult Christian education by attending a "parish life conference" led by William M. Baxter, then rector of St. Mark's Church on Capitol Hill in Washington, D.C. When I called to ask if I could attend one of his weekend conferences, Bill replied that he would not accept me as a participant but that I could join him as a member of the staff. My only responsibility would be to participate in two role plays, taking the part of a successful businessman who had lost all meaning in his life.

The first evening of the conference, I found I had no difficulty in playing the role of someone whose life had no meaning. Before ten minutes had passed, I realized that I was not play-acting but allowing my true self to emerge, the self I had suppressed during three years of theological education and a year of ordained ministry. What was most troubling about this discovery was that I could hear myself speaking in the voices all around me as the members of the group told me that I should have faith. Their words sounded so hollow. The people speaking the words seemed so false. Only once during the role play did anyone say anything that struck me as genuine. Jake Thrower, in real life a retired milkman, had told me that if I would believe in God and accept Jesus Christ as my savior, I would be all right, but when I asked if he really believed that, he replied simply, "Nah." His answer touched me, and strangely enough, calmed the inner turmoil I was experiencing.

After a whole day of reflecting on their initial exercise at the conference, my group of "friends" were to meet me for the second role play. This time around, the staff had given them a choice of circumstances for the meeting. The group set the stage for the role play by announcing that the meeting would take place in the waiting room of the local hospital. They had decided that my wife had been in a nearly fatal automobile accident and that the blood they had donated had saved her life. Apparently they thought they could coerce me into being grateful for their help. They were no longer eagerly helpful, doing their Christian duty. Instead, they had become mean and spiteful, dominated by the anger they felt toward me for refusing all the help they had so generously offered. When I did not accept the meaning of life they held out to me—that is, when I did not agree to become like them—they turned against me. I knew that this was just a play, an educational exercise, but I was sickened by the thought that they were so angry they chosen a scene involving the death of my wife.

On Sunday morning, at the celebration of the Holy Communion that concluded the conference, Bill Baxter turned to me and said, "Adams, preach." I opened my mouth to speak, but no words came. My eyes were not so withholding. The tears began to flow as if they would never stop. They were tears of sorrow for all I had lost—the beliefs I had so carefully constructed and my strong sense of certainty. But they were also tears of relief. I no longer had to pretend to be what I was not; God accepted me with all my doubts, my questions, and my skepticism. Many years later I came across Isaac of Syria's observation about prayer: "If your eyes become filled with tears, and tears run freely down your cheeks, then know that the barrier before you has begun to break down."[1] From my experience that Sunday morning, I knew exactly what St. Isaac meant.

In the years that have followed my Sunday morning outpouring, I have tried my best to say only what I believe and to avoid putting myself under any pressure to believe what does not make sense to me. Although much of John's gospel still offends me, I found in the eighth chapter an observation attributed to Jesus that has been my guiding principle: "You will know the truth, and the truth will make you free." In the original Greek of the gospel the word for truth is *aletheia*, a word that begins with the negative particle "a." *Aletheia* originally meant "that which is not hidden or not forgotten." That weekend I "told the truth" in the original Greek sense of the word, and the truth set me free. My inability to believe what I thought I was supposed to believe was no longer hidden or forgotten.

Although I assumed that other Christians might think that I was unfit to be an ordained minister, I found encouragement for my rediscovered commitment to spiritual honesty in some of the things that other clergymen were writing at the time. John Robinson's *Honest to God* and Paul van Buren's *The Secular Meaning of the Gospel* helped me to stay on the course that I had set for myself: the pursuit of truth. For the most part, however, I found more affinity with the laity than with the clergy.

When I began speaking in churches around the country after the publication of my first book, *So You Think You're Not Religious?*, I asked the people who had gathered to hear me how many of them had similar doubts and questions. Although I did not take an accurate count, I think I would be safe in saying that on the average about three-fourths of them put up their hands. Admittedly, these were groups of people who had selected themselves to attend because of their interest in my point of view, but they proved to me that our churches today have many questioning people like me.

Most of them were my age or older. To find out what had happened to the next generation, at these gatherings I asked a follow-up question: "How many of you have adult children who no longer go to church?" Once again I was confronted with a forest of raised hands. Younger people with a perspective similar to mine and to that of their parents have many different reasons for dropping out of the church, but some of them may have come to the conclusion that because of their beliefs, or the lack of them, they are not acceptable candidates for membership in a Christian community. From what my audiences have told me, I have come to the conclusion that few of these younger people ever had an open and frank discussion about religion with their parents or with other significant adults. They grew up thinking everyone at church believed all those things that seemed so implausible by the time they reached college age.

Questioning people who have stayed with the church need to find some new ways of talking about their religion to those outside the church, even their own children, if they hope to bring them into their ranks. Other Christians, those who by their natures do not feel compelled to think about matters of faith, also may need to find new ways of interpreting their heritage if they want to open the doors of the church to those who cannot help asking questions. When church members try to welcome more people into their congregations, they must ask themselves, "Do we want to include those who will insist on talking about their doubts?" I have written this book in the hope that it will contribute to a strategy of evangelism for those who can answer yes to that question.

Part One

Chapter 1

The Limits of
Conventional Evangelism

66 "The Episcopalian Goes the Way of the Dodo" trumpeted a 1990 headline in the *Wall Street Journal.* The story that followed was not exactly news to church leaders in mainline American Protestant denominations. They were all too aware that not only the Episcopalians were slipping: the Methodists, who had once accounted for fourteen percent of the population, had dropped to nine, and the Presbyterians from six percent to three. Distressed by three decades of declining membership, many denominational leaders had already begun to promote an activity they called evangelism. After the Congregational Christian Church and the Evangelical and Reformed Church merged in 1957 and saw their combined membership fall from 2.2 million to 1.6 million by 1990, they launched "evangelism institutes" to teach their members how to promote church growth. Similarly, the Episcopal Church, after suffering a decline of a million members, in 1990 launched a "decade of evangelism."

Although each organization has its own definition of evangelism, what Episcopalians say they mean by the term represents a fairly typical interpretation and illustrates the limitations that churches have imposed on their ability to grow. They define evangelism as "the presentation of Jesus Christ, in the power of the Holy Spirit, in such ways that persons may be led to believe in Him as Savior and follow Him as Lord within the fellowship of His Church."[1] This definition may seem like a harmless use of religious language to dignify a term that Christians use when they mean "recruit new members," but both the word "evangelism" and its theological explanation have a way of restricting a church's ability to grow.

Definitions of evangelism have a way of contributing to the negative attitudes attached to the word. The emphasis on believing suggests that the purpose of the enterprise is to convert people from one set of beliefs, which are wrong or misguided, to a belief in Jesus, which is the only correct form of believing. The suggestion that "the power of the Holy Spirit" backs Jesus in the competition for religious affiliation gives Christians an air of superiority that outsiders experience as arrogant and unattractive. Even people with some attachment to Christianity have found themselves questioning the church's claim to a unique and exclusive revelation. People in my age group may have developed a questioning attitude under the influence of existentialism in the years following the Second World War, but many younger people, those in the so-called baby-boom generation, apparently have the same sort of questions. Dean Hoge, Benton Johnson, and Donald Luidens did a study of Presbyterians in that age group, now between thirty-three and forty-two years old, as well as of those now forty-three to fifty-two, the ones they call the "Pre-Boomer sample." They reported their findings in a book, *Vanishing Boundaries: The Religion of Mainline Protestant Baby Boomers.* One of their conclusions came as no surprise to me. Over two-thirds of those who have left the church do not agree "that the absolute truth for humankind is in Jesus Christ."[2]

Perceptive people cannot help but notice that Muslims, Jews, Buddhists, Hindus, and adherents of Native American religions also seem to have access to God. If the churches insist on their claim that Christianity is "truer" than other religions, they will automatically exclude not only half the people who have left the church but the vast majority of those who never have belonged.

Another reason that conventional evangelism has such limited possibilities is that so many people have absolutely no interest in getting involved with any activity known as "evangelism." For them the word itself has mostly negative connotations. Until the middle of the twentieth century the word was perfectly respectable, developing from a New Testament term, *euangelion,* a combination of the Greek words for good and message. The English word "gospel" evolved from "godspell," an ancient translation of *euangelion* that combined early forms of "good" and "spiel," the latter being a common expression for any sort of discourse. Evangelism, then, originally meant simply the business of communicating the good message, telling people how the Jesus story could make a positive difference in their lives.

While the New Testament does not actually mention evangelism, certain people are called evangelists. The Acts of the Apostles includes a story of Paul and his companions staying at the house of Philip the evangelist. The Letter to the Ephesians includes evangelists among those who have received particular divine gifts—the others being apostles, prophets, pastors, and teachers. The author of the letter we know as Second Timothy urged the recipient to "do the work of an evangelist." Apparently in the early years of the church, evangelism was the function assigned to particular individuals who had an aptitude for that sort of work.

Resistance to Evangelism Within the Church

Most churchgoing Christians have a vague idea that evangelism has some connection to what the King James Version of the Bible calls the "gospel" and modern English translations call the "good news," but most often they are reminded of a particular approach to Christianity that emphasizes the constant recruitment of new members. Before examining the limited effectiveness of conventional evangelism with those outside the church, we need to understand why so many church members resist all efforts to win their support for an evangelistic enterprise.

In spite of the biblical basis for evangelism, many practicing Christians have objected to proposals by their denominational leaders that they get involved with evangelism at the local level. Trouble with the concept of evangelism among church members developed in modern times when individuals who called themselves evangelists appeared on the scene, preaching first at tent meetings and subsequently on radio and television. Many of these evangelists have been honest and dedicated people, but enough have been charlatans and frauds to give evangelism a bad name. They have shamelessly played on the fears of the gullible to enrich themselves, promised miraculous cures for a price, and offered unlimited happiness to those willing to pay. The most clever and skillful of the lot have made a fortune from the business of evangelism, and some—Jim Bakker, for example—have used illegal as well as unethical means for enriching themselves. Others have used their popularity to build a political power base; Pat Robertson and Jerry Falwell often seem more interested in politics than in ministry. By their behavior, evangelists have so tarnished the word that many Christians cannot bear to use it.

Even the most honest and dedicated of the modern evangelists have created a problem for many Christians through preaching that appeals directly to the emotions of their audience. Appealing to emotions does not constitute an offense—music and drama do the same—but the presentations of the evangelists, unlike those of composers and playwrights, tend to be decidedly anti-intellectual. Many evangelists are fundamentalists; they quote from the Bible as if it were an accurate source of historical and scientific knowledge. Even evangelists who do not hold to the scientific and historical accuracy of everything printed in the Bible pitch their message primarily to people not trained to think for themselves, putting off anyone who values independent thinking and intellectual curiosity.

The anti-intellectual position of the popular evangelists has convinced many college-educated Christians that evangelism is a lower-class phenomenon. Those from families who are only a generation or two up from the working poor often react with an instinctive negativity to any activity that threatens to identify them with a way of life that their families were only too happy to leave behind. One could argue that no proper Christian should be concerned about class distinctions, but such an argument would not alter the fact that many members of the so-called mainline churches have an unconscious, but pronounced, class bias.

Closely associated with class are matters of taste, but class and taste do not always go hand in hand. To some extent, taste follows geography. Evangelists appear to be more popular in the south than in the northeast, with a greater following in small towns and rural areas than in major cities. They can find an audience more easily between the Rockies and the Alleghenies than they can on either coast. Because taste plays such a large part in developing an identity, many urban Christians would no more be inclined to get involved with evangelism than they would to appear in what California mystery writer Sue Grafton refers to as a "full Cleveland"—a polyester suit with white shoes and a white belt. In short, Christians with any tendency toward snobbishness are likely to think that evangelism is a tasteless business.

Christians have another reason to stereotype evangelism when they turn to the political news and see how frequently evangelists ally themselves with the extreme right, such as conservative parents who do not want their children to learn about evolution in the public schools or ask that schools teach the biblical view of creation as a reasonable alternative. The involvement of evangelists in political controversies provides yet another reason why Christians, especially those of a more liberal political persuasion, have difficulty developing much enthusiasm for anything connected with evangelism.

Objections to the involvement of the TV evangelists in political controversies rest on a foundation that has more substance than mere political preference. In most of the controversies the evangelists take a position that, from a liberal perspective, comes across as conservative, narrow, and mean-spirited. The evangelists' denunciation of gay men and lesbians seems motivated more by hate than by love for their neighbors. Their attitude toward women with unwanted pregnancies suggests that they have none of the compassion demonstrated by the one they profess to be their Lord and Savior. Their opposition to controlling the purchase of hand guns implies that they favor violence over peace. Their insistence that the United States is supposed to be a Christian nation betrays a dangerous bigotry toward people of other faiths, especially Jews. To the liberal observer, when the evangelists enter the political arena they usually side with the forces of intolerance and oppression. It is no wonder that many Christians have reached the conclusion that evangelism has distorted and corrupted the gospel of Jesus Christ.

Evangelism and Institutional Survival

Because modern evangelists have given evangelism such a bad reputation—especially among well-educated, urban, politically liberal Christians—the emphasis church leaders have placed on evangelism appears to be a mistake. Try as they will to promote evangelism among their congregations, the hierarchies of the major denominations are not likely to inspire much enthusiasm for any program that carries a name with so many offensive connotations. To make matters worse, many parish clergy and lay leaders harbor a basic mistrust of their denominational hierarchy's motives for promoting evangelism. The great interest in evangelism appears to come not out of a concern for human beings who live without hope, but out of an anxiety about dwindling numbers. The more church membership declines as a percentage of the population, the more interest church leaders show in evangelism. In each of the major denominations, the factions promoting evangelism seem to have convinced the policy-makers that they know how to save the church from a continuing decline in membership.

When national leaders representing the older, more open traditions seized on the concept of evangelism, they were not thinking about all the negative connotations that their constituents attached to the word because of the radio and television evangelists, but about the success of churches that call themselves "evangelical." Unlike some of the other denominations, the evangelical churches were not suffering a decline in membership and in many instances were actually growing, which is why denominations such as the Episcopal Church, which had once emphasized open inquiry and acceptance of different perspectives, were drawn to the single-minded approach of the evangelicals. In its 1991 report, the Evangelism Commission of the Episcopal Church stressed the importance of decision and conversion, with an emphasis on a "personal commitment to Jesus Christ."[3]

Those church leaders who have taken a stand in favor of evangelism, however, are meeting resistance from their constituencies. The first aspect of the problem created by the push for evangelism becomes apparent every time the national church headquarters sends out another proposal for promoting evangelism; clergy are likely to disregard it as simply more propaganda heaped on them by denominational bureaucrats. The other aspect of resistance to evangelism at the local level is more serious, and it appears in the attitude most congregations have toward their own growth. Unless they are facing the question of actual survival, most of the members do not want their churches to grow.

In a congregation of one hundred members, the pastor heard people complaining that the church had been spoiled by all the new people; they now had so many people coming to the early service that they could no longer fit at the tables available for breakfast. The complaint of the old-timers at this little church sounds amusingly similar to the grumbling of the parishioners in a church with three thousand members on the rolls: because of the new people, they can't find a place to park the car, and they can't get a good seat without arriving at least ten minutes before the service.

People who do not want their churches to grow can sometimes put aside their disdain for the hierarchy long enough to take comfort from the discovery that their denomination's commitment to evangelism does not actually require them to recruit new members. For example, an official bulletin of the Episcopal Church that includes statistics on church growth manages to state what "evangelism includes" without ever mentioning the desirability of increasing the membership.[4] People who do not want their congregations to grow may be pleased to find a justification for retaining their exclusive, club-like atmosphere, but of course they may never admit it.

Another factor national leaders have failed to consider is the impact their program of evangelism would have on the newest members in their congregations. Many people who have joined mainline churches as adults spent their years as children attending conservative churches. Ask for a show of hands in almost any urban Episcopal, Presbyterian, or United Church of Christ congregation and see for yourself how many members grew up in conservative Protestant or Roman Catholic churches. According to a survey made by Wade Clark Roof, a professor at the University of California at Santa Barbara, and reported in his book *A Generation of Seekers*, seven percent of the people who grew up in conservative congregations have now affiliated with mainline churches.[5] Many of them are clear that they could not stay with a religious organization that makes exclusive claims about access to God. News reports, such as the following on the refusal of certain groups to attend the second Parliament of the World's Religions, confirm them in their choice of a more open-minded tradition:

> The Southern Baptist Convention, for instance, is among the groups that declined to send a representative. Many evangelical and fundamentalist Christians believe that such gatherings are at best a dis-

traction from spreading the Gospel and at worst a confusing compromise of their belief that Christianity is the only way to salvation.[6]

Many members of mainline churches dropped out of more conservative churches when they went off to college. When they reached their late twenties or early thirties and decided they wanted an association with a Christian community for their own sakes or for their children, they consciously sought out a congregation that would hear their questions and tolerate their doubts. To such recent arrivals, the talk of evangelism sounds particularly threatening, especially to those who choose a congregation because it seems like a healthier and more open-minded community than the one they rejected as soon as they were out from under the control of their parents.

I do not mean to suggest that people who have left conservative churches have only negative memories about their early religious experience, because if they did not have some pleasant associations, I doubt if they would have sought a Christian congregation of any sort when they grew up. Garrison Keillor—a favorite among National Public Radio listeners for his "Prairie Home Companion"—recounted some of the positive aspects of belonging to a fundamentalist church that was "too small to be called Evangelical." As a child he had known that he and his family were conspicuously different from everyone else, but he also had felt very secure: "We were so separated from the world with our restrictions and discipline that it encouraged us to have a greater love for each other." Keillor even had a kind word to say about evangelists:

> Evangelists are almost always deeply flawed people. Their passion comes out of their flaws. I can believe the stories that I hear about lust, adultery, and the general screwing around that goes on in the world of Evangelism. To me, it makes perfect sense. If Evangelists are able to live with their flaws, it somehow enables them to do what they do.[7]

Although the evangelical churches are growing while the others are struggling simply to maintain their present numbers, relatively few people have taken a spiritual path in the opposite direction from that chosen by Garrison Keillor, who left a conservative church to become an Episcopalian. You do not need the results of polls and sociological studies to know what has happened to dropouts from mainline churches: most of them have not become evangelicals or pentecostals. According to Roof's survey, only twelve percent of the dropouts have joined more conservative Protestant churches, while forty-four percent of them now have no religious affiliation.[8] These are the people who have attended Sunday schools of mainline congregations and have belonged to their youth groups. Then they leave home. The ones who go to college learn about the sordid history of Christianity: the brutality of the crusades, the horrors of the Inquisition, the scandal of the divided papacy, the burning of heretics, and the endless wars fought among Christians of different persuasions. The change in sexual mores, the anti-establishment bias, and the emphasis on personal freedom that they find in college makes the church of their childhood seem irrelevant. They find themselves in an atmosphere that encourages intellectual curiosity. If they have never done so before, they start asking questions about ultimate concerns. The answers they learned in Sunday school do not fit with the new information they are acquiring and the new ways of thinking they are developing. They stop going to church, except for holidays when they are home with their families. Because they no longer can recite the creed without choking on the words, these occasional visits to the church convince them that they cannot be church members without being hypocrites.

By embracing conventional evangelism, therefore, mainline churches may make an unintentional decision to write off their own children. They have made returning to church a difficult if not impossible choice for all their offspring who have serious questions about their tradition. The loss of a great portion of the younger generation to secularism has demonstrated one of conventional evangelism's most critical limitations. Unfortunately, church leaders fail to calculate the possible impact on their own younger people when they downplay their distinctive traditions in favor of conventional evangelism. They also fail to note that the conservative churches do not have a much better record than the mainline churches when it comes to holding the loyalty of their young people. In Roof's survey, thirty-six percent of the people who grew up in conservative churches currently have no religious affiliation.

According to Gallup polls, the most rapidly growing, religiously identifiable group in the United States is the non-affiliated, which went from being two percent of the population in the early 1950s to nine percent in 1990 and eleven percent two years later. This group consists of people who have religious interests and longings but cannot accept the demands and dogmas they associate with Christianity. Many of them resemble a person I will call Rob, who dropped out of Sunday school when he was twelve years old. The only information he has received about Christianity since has come from television and newspapers. Most of what he sees and hears about Christianity comes through reports on the scandalous behavior and the political maneuvering of theologically conservative clergy. Rob assumes that Christians exist who are different from the ones he reads about in the newspapers and sees on television, but what he has learned from the media has shaped what he thinks of Christianity.

News stories about the power that charismatic religious leaders like Jim Jones and David Koresh exercise over their followers have also had an impact on Rob's views of the church. As far as he can see, the more enthusiastic and single-minded the followers of any religious leader become, the more dangerous they will be to themselves or the people around them. Seeing what happens to Christian communities that suppress doubt and permit no questions, Rob has come to the conclusion that unswerving faith produces dangerous consequences. He hopes that his churchgoing next-door neighbors have more sense than the fanatical followers of charismatic Christian leaders, but assumes they have the same certainty about the truth and leave no room for doubt in their religion.

Now imagine Rob's response if his neighbor tries to engage him in conversation about accepting Jesus Christ as his personal Lord and Savior. When any church member picks up the evangelistic style, an outsider like Rob will have more reason than ever to lump all Christians together and to distrust the lot. By claiming that they represent the absolute truth and that they know God's will, the churches forfeit whatever credibility and respectability they might have had and reinforce the prejudices any outsider might harbor against Christianity. Even if conventional evangelism does not evoke these fears, the language typical of an evangelistic approach to Christianity probably would be enough to keep them far away from church. I wonder how often the promoters of evangelism ever stop to think about the impact of their words on those people who, by their very natures, have to think for themselves.

In its cruder manifestations, conventional evangelism also has a way of emphasizing what is wrong with people. While the most sensitive evangelists attempt to affirm their listeners, from the mouths of the less enlightened the message often comes across, "You are sick and sinful. Listen to us and you can become healthy and righteous." This approach may appeal to people who have never thought very highly of themselves, but people with a healthy self-regard will not be interested in associating with a group dedicated to the proposition that God loves only those human beings who confess to being miserable sinners. A person with any degree of skepticism about the value of organized religion may hear all the talk about sin and come to the conclusion that those doing the talking have a problem, an unhealthy obsession with what they like least about themselves.

Perhaps the most troublesome words in the language of evangelism are demands related to faith and believing. "You must believe that Jesus Christ is the son of God." "You have to take some things on faith." Such admonitions to a person with a skeptical nature are about as helpful as telling blind people that they should see. Recent studies have shown that people who are born blind, or who lose their sight in childhood, cannot see in the way that other people do even if their sight is restored. Their brains no longer have the capacity to process and make sense of the great influx of data coming through the optic nerves. In a similar fashion, people born without the capacity to believe what they are told, or who lose the capacity through early experience, cannot be made to see the world in the same way that believers do. To those who cannot believe, the message of evangelism appears to be: "If you do not believe, you have a wicked and perverse nature." People with questioning minds feel they must remain outsiders unless they can become something other than what they are. The result of the emphasis on evangelism has been for more and more denominations to pitch their message exclusively to the people with an inborn capacity for believing while ignoring the other half of the population, who find believing difficult.

Evangelism Redefined

Evangelism has so many negative associations for so many practicing Christians as well as for outsiders that the church might be better off if everyone could agree to banish the concept. Both the word and the brand of Christianity it represents have stood in the way of many churches attracting new members. By relinquishing all claims to evangelism, however, mainline churches would allow the concept and the practice to become the undisputed property of the evangelicals. Evangelism has deep roots in the Bible, and we are unlikely to find a better word for what the first Christians had in mind when they wrote about *euangelion*, the good message.

If we are going to use the word "evangelism," we will need a new definition that will convey an open attitude toward religious doubt and intellectual curiosity. We will need to qualify the term to avoid the stance of spiritual superiority that conventional evangelism suggests. We will need a concept of evangelism that accepts the validity of other religious traditions.

We can reclaim evangelism by defining it as *church members letting outsiders in on what they have found of value in Christianity.* Evangelism happens when members of the church are so convinced that God has enriched their lives through their participation in the life of a Christian community that they want to include other people in what they have found to be valuable. Through evangelism Christians express delight in having found that church participation helps with the business of trying to make sense out of their lives. Evangelism suggests an attitude of spiritual generosity as opposed to a posture of spiritual penury, trying to hoard the gifts of God for the exclusive use of the present members. Even congregations with a strong aversion to evangelism, as they understand the concept, probably do not want to think of themselves as spiritually stingy. If they learn that evangelism is a matter of being generous, they might be more open to the idea.

Spiritually generous neighbors might be able to find common ground with someone like Rob. In the first place, they would be putting into practice the best they know about how to treat each other in their own households. Secondly, they would be good neighbors, attending to all the little things that make a neighborhood work:

making sure that their children do not leave skateboards and bikes on the public sidewalks, putting out their trash cans on collection day, taking over a casserole when Rob's wife is in the hospital with a new baby. Next, they would introduce the ethical and spiritual dimensions of any subject in casual conversations, being careful to avoid religious jargon in what they say. Finally, they would find ways of letting Rob know that their church is a good place for asking questions and exploring doubts. If they sensed any openness at all, they might invite him to a church event: a lecture, a concert, or even a worship service.

When a congregation redefines evangelism in terms of generosity, they also may remind themselves that the followers of Jesus have a tradition of hospitality, a willingness to keep membership in their communities open to everyone who could profit from belonging. They would go out of their way to welcome people without regard for their capacity to believe. They would not be offended if a visitor said, "I'm not sure I should be here since I don't believe in the divinity of Jesus, and I'm not sure what I really believe about God." Instead, they would respond, "Lots of us in the church are not at all sure about what we can believe, but we think we're getting somewhere by asking questions." Most church people would want to make outsiders welcome if they thought about the implications, for they would not want to describe themselves as deliberately exclusive any more than they would want to think of themselves as spiritually stingy. If they can understand that in the Christian tradition being evangelistic is the opposite of stinginess and exclusivity, they might learn to tolerate the idea in spite of its negative connotations.

With a new toleration for the concept of evangelism might also come the realization that one indicator of a generous attitude in the congregation is an increase in membership. If the members of the church are genuinely open to letting other people in on their experience, other people will want to be included. Still, those who talk about evangelism must be careful to avoid leaving the impression that an increase in membership constitutes the only indicator of an evangelistic attitude. The demographics of some areas preclude the possibility of significant growth in numbers. For a congregation in a town with a declining population and a high percentage of retired people, a stable membership may not indicate a stingy and exclusive attitude any more than the rapid growth of a congregation in a new suburb with lots of young families moving in means a generous and inclusive spirit. The unavoidable fact remains, however, that growth in membership represents one indicator of a congregation's attitude. Clergy and congregations who say that evangelism is not about numbers but about quality of faith may unconsciously be trying to disguise their stinginess with lofty words.

In making sure that their definition of the term includes church growth as an indicator of attitude, those in favor of intelligent evangelism also must insist that the purpose of the church is not to recruit new members whose job will be to recruit more members. By promoting evangelism they are not advocating a hard sell or the use of coercive tactics. Evangelism became a dirty word partly because church groups turned an indicator into a purpose, confusing sign with substance. To concentrate on church growth as an end in itself is as foolish as taking cold baths for a temperature of 103° instead of going to the doctor. Taking a temperature can provide valuable information for the physician making a diagnosis, but the doctor will look for the cause rather than treat the temperature. In the same fashion, attendance records can reveal a great deal about the health of a congregation, but an attempt to boost attendance in the name of evangelism without examining the congregation's basic attitudes and behavior will usually prove to be counterproductive.

All too often in evangelistic outreach the most basic attitudes of a congregation go unexamined. Congregations can easily become exclusive or closed in on themselves without realizing what attitudes are conditioning their behavior. They do not realize that either refusing to engage in evangelism or adopting a program of conventional evangelism may produce the same effect: the creation of exclusive congregations. A congregation that makes no effort at evangelism can develop unconscious standards of exclusivity, and a congregation with a program of conventional evangelism can easily exclude anyone with serious doubts or questions. Before a congregation can make any headway with a serious reexamination of its stance in regard to evangelism, the members of the church will have to face these issues.

Chapter 2

A Feast for All Peoples

A compelling vision of the way the world ought to be appears in a psalm that has been preserved among the prophesies of Isaiah:

> On this mountain the LORD of hosts will make for all peoples a feast of rich food, a feast of well-aged wines, of rich food filled with marrow, of well-aged wines strained clear. (Isaiah 25:6)

Isaiah's poem draws a picture of a banquet that most people would be delighted to attend. This will be a sumptuous meal at which calories do not count and cholesterol is no one's concern. The host will provide the finest wine, not the sort that comes in gallon jugs, but at least the equivalent of a vintage Mouton Rothschild. In this vision of a perfect banquet, God appears as the host. And who are the honored guests? Not just the people of Israel, the chosen people, but *all peoples*.

Some passages in the Hebrew scriptures picture God favoring the people of Israel over all others, but this passage from Isaiah emphasizes God's concern for every human being. The implications are troubling for people who think that they have a special relationship with God; if they are not special by definition, on what basis can they trust God to support them when they feel threatened? As the poem unfolds, God appears to welcome both the oppressed and their oppressors:

> Then the LORD GOD will wipe away the tears from all faces, and the disgrace of his people he will take away from all the earth, for the LORD has spoken. (v. 8)

Those in sorrow are especially welcome, but so are those who are in disgrace. The Hebrew word here translated as "disgrace" means to be exposed or shamed. People who live in disgrace have had their weaknesses or failures exposed for all to see. They can feel the contempt with which others look at them. The tears of people in disgrace are expressions of both grief and rage, feelings that easily turn to hatred and explode in violence. Palestinians in the Gaza Strip or African Americans in Los Angeles have displayed the fury of people who can no longer tolerate the contempt of their more affluent neighbors. According to Isaiah, God will wipe away the tears and take away the disgrace. Their grief and shame will be removed; all people will come to the table as equals and as friends, and will enjoy the meal together in peace.

Something seems to be wrong with this picture. Why is God making no demands? Are there no standards by which people qualify for an invitation? God has established no test for right thinking, correct beliefs, or proper behavior. Consequently, no individual or group can claim to be special, a situation that may reduce the invitation's appeal.

The Great Commission

Whoever wrote the closing lines of Matthew's gospel seems to have caught the inclusive spirit of the feast described by Isaiah. Its author used similar language: "Go therefore and make disciples of all nations, baptizing them in the name of the Father and of the Son and of the Holy Spirit." The Greek word *ethnoi*, here translated "nations," has much the same meaning as the Hebrew word translated "peoples" in the poem about the great feast. Obviously the followers of Jesus could not baptize nations, as such, but they could offer to include all kinds of people. They were not to exclude anyone.

Given the natural human desire for exclusivity, the willingness of Jesus's disciples to report that their teacher wanted to exclude no one indicates that Jesus himself held out the possibility that his followers did not have to take refuge in exclusive groups. Unfortunately, communities organized in the name of Jesus have often turned out to be much like all other groups that people join in order to feel that they belong and that they matter. The exclusive nature of the church itself saves them from their fear of being nothing. Although they may talk about God, their security comes from being a part of a group that defines itself by emphasizing how its members are different from other people. The difference that defines a church may be primarily ethnic or cultural, but in homogeneous societies the separating factor is belief. People who believe understand themselves to be different from doubters, skeptics, and agnostics. Although they would not say so, those who believe see themselves as superior to those who do not.

The need to feel that we are saved, and are therefore special, may arise as a way of fortifying ourselves to live in the face of our deepest fear, the fear that we are no one and count for nothing. The dread of being of no consequence drives so much of human behavior that the vision of a universal invitation to God's banquet had little chance of gaining popularity among Christians who wanted to make belief the requirement for belonging.

Varieties of Skepticism

I think of belief and unbelief in the same way that I do music; even with the best of training, not all people can learn to play the piano well. When I was in the fifth grade, our local school board hired a beautiful young woman, Miss Whitemore, to be our music teacher. As soon as I learned that Miss Whitemore was taking on private piano students, I implored my parents to let me take lessons from her. They agreed, and from that time on I was a diligent piano student. Every day I practiced the lessons from *Teaching Little Fingers to Play* that Miss Whitemore assigned, and as I practiced I eagerly looked forward to my hour alone with her and hoped earnestly for her approval. At the end of the academic year, Miss Whitemore informed my parents that they were wasting their money on piano lessons for me; I appeared to have no talent for music. I was crushed, but I learned an important lesson about human possibilities and limitations. I am convinced that one can no more make a skeptic out of a person with an inborn talent for believing than one can turn a born skeptic into a believer.

Skepticism appears in a variety of forms, and skeptics handle their questions in a variety of ways. Most of them will not come inside a church building except for a special event, such as a wedding or a concert, but others may attend worship services every week all the while feeling emotionally and spiritually excluded from the core of the community's life.

Among the great variety of skeptics in the world, the type that a church member may be least likely to encounter is the total skeptic, but understanding him or her can help practicing Christians recognize the skepticism that surfaces at times in nearly everyone. Total skeptics doubt, question, or disagree with anything they cannot verify. They should not be confused with atheists, who must be understood as a type of true believer. Atheists do not question the existence of God; they believe passionately that God does not exist. Many people expressed surprise when Bill Murray—the son of Madalyn Murray O'Hair, America's most outspoken atheist—became a Baptist and then an evangelist, but on close examination his move was not so surprising. Now in open rebellion against his mother, who had made him the center of the Supreme Court test on prayers in public schools, he has simply transferred his allegiance from one absolute belief system to another. A total skeptic could no more be an atheist than a fundamentalist.

Total skeptics question everything and everybody. They will doubt reports of scientific investigations as readily as they will challenge the programs put forward by politicians. When scientists warn of the disastrous effects in store for the world because of global warming, they will be among the first to recall that only a few years ago scientists were terrifying the public with predictions of a new ice age. When a candidate for president talks about reducing the deficit while increasing spending for either defense or economic stimulation, they will quickly point out the mathematical impossibility of the proposals. Naturally, their skepticism extends to the realm of religion as well. They cannot accept any report of an event in which the known laws of nature were somehow suspended. Stories about miracles must be dismissed as absurd. Accounts of the virgin birth and the resurrection of Jesus from the dead must be put in the same category as descriptions of visitors from outer space.

In spite of their doubts about much in the Christian tradition, total skeptics sometimes have wistful feelings about the church. They
may feel attracted by the music and the drama of the liturgy. They
may experience a sense of consolation at the funeral of a friend.
They may admire the intellectual vigor of authors, such as T. S. Eliot
and Walker Percy, who have written from the perspective of convinced Christians. But they think that they cannot participate in
worship without compromising their integrity. When they voice complaints about church people, they will say that they cannot stand the
hypocrisy of most Christians whose behavior does not measure up to
their professed beliefs. Total skeptics fear that by taking part in
Christian rituals they will appear to be endorsing a set of beliefs
they may not hold and that, as a consequence, they will be as guilty
of hypocrisy as the insincere Christians whom they despise.

Total skeptics can be exasperating to people for whom belief
comes easily, especially since they appear to have made a religion of
their skepticism. Skeptics can become dogmatic in their insistence
that "there are no answers" and have a way of looking down on people who do not enjoy questioning, probing, and arguing. In order to
avoid feeling defensive, those who wish to welcome skeptics into
their churches would do well to remember that total skeptics have
the same need as everybody else to cope with their fear of nothingness. The more absolute and dogmatic they become in their skepticism, the more insecure they are probably feeling.

Although total skeptics can be difficult, people who are skeptical
only about religious matters may present an even greater challenge
for the church member committed to making disciples of all people.
Religious skeptics may show little concern for facts and proofs in all
other areas of life. One Texan who scoffed at everything connected
with organized religion confided to his physician that he ate a great
quantity of cartilage to prevent arthritis. The old rancher could not
recall where he had picked up the idea that eating cartilage pre-
vented arthritis, but nothing the doctor said could shake his belief in
the efficacy of his peculiar diet. Religion was another matter. He remembered a great deal of what he had been told as a child and believed none of it.

Many people whose skepticism is limited to religion developed
their doubts at an early age, often because of the treatment they re-

ceived at the hands of the clergy or because of the way their parents used religion to control them. The pastor of a church with a predominantly gay and lesbian membership told me that a majority of the members had stayed away from churches for years because of the way church people had insulted and demeaned everyone attracted to others of the same sex. Many homosexuals have suffered physical punishment as well as rejection. The pastor called this kind of treatment "religious abuse."

At an Alcoholics Anonymous meeting where the topic of discussion was the eleventh of the twelve steps, a young woman said that whenever she feels God's presence she finds it necessary "to push God away." She traced her problems with God to her early experiences in church. What she heard from the pulpit was that she was a miserable sinner, unable to do right in the eyes of God. Her mother reinforced that message of unredeemable guilt by slapping the child and even hitting her with a hymnal whenever she squirmed in the pew. As is the case with many people in Twelve Step programs, she did not object to meeting in a church conference room, but she would never enter the place of worship.

Perhaps a less formidable challenge than the religious skeptic is the type that I have classified as the partial skeptic. A former senior warden of my parish pointed out to me that most people are not totally skeptical about everything, nor even totally skeptical about just religious matters. Instead, they easily believe some things, such as the existence of God and even life after death, but at the same time they have serious doubts about the reliability of the Bible. They may balk at the idea of Joshua causing the sun to stand still or of Jesus changing water into wine, or they may have serious questions about the circumstances surrounding the birth of Jesus and about his resurrection from the dead.

Partial skeptics consider themselves to be Christians and even claim a denomination when checking into a hospital, but they may stay away from church out of the same fear of hypocrisy that influences total skeptics. Others have decided that they will live with a little hypocrisy in order to find what the church has to offer. The bolder ones ask questions and are vocal about their doubts while the more timid, perhaps those most afraid of rejection, keep their questions and doubts pretty much to themselves. Convinced Christians at least have the possibility of finding common ground for conversation with partial skeptics, whether they are in or outside of the church. The belief in God and respect for Jesus that they hold in common can provide a starting place.

Once when I was setting up a speaking tour in the Carolinas I called a colleague in Raleigh and asked him if he would be willing to set up a meeting to discuss ministry among skeptics. After a few moments hesitation, he said no, he didn't think such a meeting would be possible. As far as he knew, there were no skeptics in Raleigh. A lawyer known to be a skeptic would have no clients; a doctor would have no patients; a real estate broker would never make a sale. Then I understood. In certain parts of the country, for someone to admit to any significant degree of skepticism about Christianity would amount to economic suicide. Church membership may not be required, but skepticism about religious matters has to be kept to oneself.

Some secret skeptics participate actively in the church, all the while suffering untold agonies of guilt for not genuinely believing what they have been taught. The mother of a woman in my congregation was a secret skeptic for most of her life. Married to a fundamentalist missionary, she spent years in remote areas of South America, working alongside her husband. After the couple had retired from the missionary field, she developed cancer. When she came to Washington for treatment, she sent word by way of her daughter that she wanted me to visit her in the hospital.

During my visit this woman told me that all of her life, even when she was trying to convert Indians in Peru, she did not believe what she was saying. She had spent her whole life trying to be a faithful Christian. She had given up everything, including family and friends, to become a missionary. She had sent her children off to boarding school when they were little more than infants so that she could continue with the Lord's work. She had suffered terribly from loneliness, the separation from her children being particularly painful. She had given everything she had, but still she had felt that she was unacceptable to God because she could not believe what she was supposed to. It was as she read my book *So You Think You're Not Religious* that she finally came to the conclusion that God loved her just as she was. She had asked to see me because she wanted to share her relief and joy with me.

As she brought her story to a close, she looked over at her husband, who sitting on the other bed. "See that man," she said to me. "He is a simple-minded believer. He can believe anything at all. I can't. And that's all there is to it." The old missionary smiled at his wife with what I took to be genuine affection, but he said nothing.

I was speechless, too, feeling almost overwhelmed by a mixture of sadness and joy. The story of her deprivation—the years wasted in the hopeless quest for God's approval, tormented by her secret doubts and questions—made me feel sadder than I could say. Yet I could not help being touched by her obvious joy at being released from the prison of silence that she had constructed to hide her skepticism.

This wife and mother who had served as a missionary tried to manage the secret of her skepticism by her strenuous devotion to what she saw as her Christian duty. In a similar fashion, many secret skeptics within the church vigorously defend orthodoxy in order to prop up their tottering belief systems. One man I encountered at a church study group demanded, Wasn't it the business of the church to strengthen people's faith and not to upset them with a lot of questions? Shouldn't the church be giving people the right answers to their questions instead of encouraging them to ask more? He continued like this for several minutes. When at last he paused for a breath, I asked him if he had ever read the gospels. He had, so I asked him if he knew of any instance when Jesus responded to a direct question with a direct answer. "No!" he shouted, with obvious anger in his voice. "And that's just the trouble!" He became thoughtful for a moment or two, and then he said quietly, "I guess that makes me a skeptic, doesn't it?"

I think it is safe to say that the people who are the most belligerent in the defense of orthodoxy are the most likely to be skeptics underneath. The tragedy for the church is that these skeptics could be the most effective missionaries to a skeptical world, if only they were not ashamed of their skepticism and knew they were acceptable in the eyes of God. Jesus taught that all people are acceptable to God; he seems to have understood that all people, those who believe as well as those who cannot, have the same longings and have to cope with the same fears.

In the novel *Presumed Innocent*, Scott Turow puts a prayer on the lips of a man being tried for a murder he did not commit:

> And now, dear God, I think dear God in whom I do not believe, I pray to you to stop this, for I am deathly frightened. Dear God, I smell my fear, with an odor as distinct as ozone on the air after a lightening flash....Dear God, dear God, I am in agony and fear, and whatever I may have done to make you bring this down upon me, release me, I pray, release me. Release me. Dear God, in whom I do not believe, dear God, let me go free.[1]

The prayer of an agnostic can be as heartfelt and genuine as the prayer of the most convinced Christian. If convinced Christians can see that such people do not stand in need of conversion—that they do not need to be changed as much as they need to be accepted—evangelism among skeptical people can become a real possibility.

Standards for Membership

If an evangelizing community decides that it is not going to require belief as a prerequisite for acceptance into the life of the church, they are immediately faced with the question: what *will* they require? Surely Christianity must have some standards. Members of the church must have some responsibility. The congregation must have some way of defining itself just to know who belongs.

Near the beginning of the second century in the present era, someone using the apostle Paul's name wrote a letter addressed to the Ephesians. Its author was caught in the tension between a recognition of God's concern for all people and the church's need to set standards for participation in its common life:

> I therefore, the prisoner in the Lord, beg you to lead a life worthy of the calling to which you have been called, with all humility and gentleness, with patience, bearing with one another in love, making every effort to maintain the unity of the Spirit in the bond of peace. There is one body and one Spirit, just as you were called to the one hope of your calling, one Lord, one faith, one baptism, one God and Father of all, who is above all and through all and in all. (Ephesians 4:1-6)

Note that the letter does not concentrate on belief but on behavior, not on what people believe, but on how they treat one another. It does view the church as an exclusive community: the only people who have a right to belong are those who are willing to be humble and gentle. Those who belong must also act with "patience," a standard that comes across more vividly in the original Greek. The word is *makrothumia*. The first part of the word suggests an extended period of time, while the second half—a metaphor taken from the term for ritual fire—meant strong feeling or passion. In other words, church members were expected to have intense feelings but to keep them under control, like a fire in a stove rather than a raging forest fire. The purpose of patience, in the original sense, comes through with the next standard: bearing with one another, or more literally "having one another up" in love. Mutual support, then, must be understood as basic to the life of the community. In addition, the church expects its members to make every effort to maintain unity and peace.

When Christians worry that admitting skeptical people will result in a "watering down of the faith," they might do well to consider what early Christian writers thought were the standards the church should uphold. If they will read through the gospels and the Acts of the Apostles and the letters written by St. Paul, they will find that the authors pay much more attention to how people treat one another than to what they believe. They will discover that the recurring theme is "Love one another," not "Believe what you are told." They also might do well to examine the standards of their own Christian community.

Outsiders are not always favorably impressed by the way church people treat one another. Some congregations—including more than a few that emphasize correct doctrine—have a reputation for being mean and quarrelsome. If such churches put aside their doctrinal disputes and concentrated on being kind to one another, according to the terms laid out in the letter to the Ephesians, two things might happen. First, they would get closer to what the early Christians meant by a life of faith, and second, they would have taken an important step in their responsibility for evangelism. When Christians treat one another decently, even agnostics are impressed. Skeptical people on the outside are going to feel drawn to the church if they observe people on the inside sustaining one another in love. Switching the emphasis from belief to behavior for the sake of evangelism, far from watering down the faith, might help a congregation find the true meaning of faith.

Besides emphasizing behavior, the passage from Ephesians also offers loyalty as a standard for belonging to a Christian community. There shall be "one Lord, one faith, one baptism." Such a pronouncement can offend certain kinds of thinking people whose curiosity has led them to an investigation of the church, but the gospel will always retain a certain offensive quality. As St. Paul wrote to the Jesus followers in Corinth, "We proclaim Christ crucified, a stumbling block to Jews and foolishness to Gentiles." Some people, especially those who have been influenced by New Age thinking, are likely to protest that one Lord, one faith, one baptism sounds much too restrictive. It sounds like the same old story, the church demanding that they subscribe to a set of beliefs as the price of admission.

In response to the protest, the evangelist can point out that the phrase is not about belief, but it does put forward loyalty as a standard of membership. For the church member there is one Lord, Jesus Christ. The search for meaning can take people in many legitimate directions, but a church member is a seeker who has decided to limit the search to the path set by Jesus of Nazareth. There is also one faith. Although the author has not qualified "faith" with a phrase beginning "in" or "that," saying that there is "one" suggests a choice among many possibilities. The letter to the Ephesians uses the Greek word for faith, *pistis,* which can mean belief but which usually means trust or confidence. To qualify for membership in a church, people must be willing to identify a connection between Jesus of Nazareth and the confidence that carries them through each day. Finally, to become a church member a person must make the affiliation public in the ritual called baptism. You can be a secret skeptic among Christians, but not a secret Christian among Christians.

The church as a human institution is an exclusive organization. To survive, the church has had to develop standards for membership, but all too often these standards have had little to do with faith and have had much more to do with race or class or capacities for belief. If a congregation fails to define its requirements for membership from a faith perspective, it will become an exclusive organization on some other basis. If church members do not emphasize loyalty to their Lord and kindness toward one another as the standards for inclusion, they will consciously or unconsciously exclude people who do not have the right clothes, or the right complexion, or the right accent, or the right way of thinking.

To make matters worse, even the most faithful standards sometimes obscure the reality of God's acceptance of all human beings. As the letter to the Ephesians put it: "There is...one God and Father of all, who is above all and through all and in all." The author of the epistle may have misunderstood some elements in the teachings of Jesus, but one aspect of Jesus's teaching comes through clearly: God is the Father of every person, watches over every person, and is in every person. People do not have to do anything to become God's children. They do not have to convert or to believe. If only all people could accept themselves as offspring of the Most High, they would not be so driven to prove that they are special. They would not have to think that their race or tribe or clan is superior to all others. They would not have to form exclusive clubs or devise ways of excluding certain types from their churches. They would understand that the way of coping with their fear of nothingness lies within themselves and not with any group to which they might belong. They are already as distinctive as they can be.

The "one God and Father of all" declaration suggests that followers of Jesus must recognize this presence of God in all people. The recognition that God is present with all people will help members of a congregation to acknowledge two related but distinct obligations. The first obligation comes into play when they encounter people who represent traditions different from their own: they will respect other points of view and other expressions of religion. They will not feel obliged to suggest that Jews or even Muslims or Buddhists or Hindus have inferior religions and stand in need of conversion. They will not have to imply that agnostics or skeptics are misguided people who should change their way of thinking. They will not claim that Jesus is the only way to God, but that Jesus is the way to God that they have chosen.

The second obligation may seem to contradict the first: all people deserve an invitation to join the community that gathers in the name of Jesus. They do not have to become Christians in order to become decent people or to know God's love, but they will be welcome if they choose to pursue their search for meaning among the followers of Jesus Christ.

One way to show respect for the people to whom we issue the invitation is to be clear with them about the obligations of membership. Understanding the cost of participating in the life of a Christian community will be particularly important for people who have had a history of problems with organized religion. They will be immediately suspicious if what they hear is: "You all come; it's all free; anything goes." Thinking people have figured out that for every promise there is a cost. They will not object to the cost, but they want to know what the church will require of them. If they accept the skeptic's dictum—"You only get what you pay for"—hearing about the responsibilities that church members voluntarily assume may intrigue them rather than put them off.

Of course, for the members of the church to be clear with potential recruits about the cost and promise of membership, they will first have to be clear with each other. They will have to figure out what the church has to offer and what the church requires of them. If they have never gone through such an exercise, a commitment to evangelism may provide just the excuse they need for doing what they should have done, especially if the commitment includes a responsibility for all the varieties of skeptical people. Any congregation can profit from the experience of putting belief aside in order to find out what loyalties and what kinds of behavior define them as a community.

Many congregations have not yet taken advantage of the opportunity for self-redefinition that goes along with a commitment to evangelism because the whole concept of evangelism is so distasteful. The members of a church are unlikely to open the door to people who are different from them until they themselves glimpse what an emphasis on thoughtful evangelism could bring to their community.

Chapter 3

The Promise of an Open Approach

W hile going through his mail one evening after work, Philip spotted a yellow flyer that intrigued him. It was an invitation to attend services at a local church, and inside he found that the flyer was aimed at people like him who had trouble accepting church doctrines. Among the reasons it gave for joining a church community, one particularly caught his eye: "Find your roots in the rituals and traditions of a people with a history." Philip realized that the flyer had been sent by a church in his neighborhood, but he had never considered going there. He had grown up in a strict fundamentalist family and had attended church faithfully until he went off to college, but once he had come to the conclusion that God was not managing the world and that life after death was highly improbable, he had decided that attending any church would be dishonest. It never occurred to him that there might be other reasons for participating in a Christian community.

The next Sunday, accompanied by his wife Mary and their little daughter, he went to the church that promised to be different from the one he had rejected as a young man. Philip and Mary received that flyer twenty years ago, and they have been active church members ever since.

The world is filled with people like Philip and Mary who think that they would have to abandon their intellectual integrity in order to be acceptable to a church. Congregations that are willing to take them as they are, without trying to convert them into believers, can grow by using a more comprehensive strategy than that usually associated with evangelism. Before they can devise and employ such a strategy, they have to decide, first, if they are willing to grow at all and, second, if they are willing to grow by accepting people like Philip and Mary into their ranks.

The resistance to growth in some congregations reflects the attitudes of their clergy; in others, it has frustrated the ambitions of their ordained ministers. Part of the problem may be that leaders, ordained or lay, have seen no promise in adding to the membership of their churches. Telling them that they should want to grow does not often produce an open attitude, nor does accusing them of being selfish and exclusive. Church leaders will never favor growth until they see a promise for themselves that will clearly outweigh the costs they fear.

Some church leaders are so opposed to acting out of pure self-interest that they fail to recognize the necessity of taking the interests of the congregation into account when they attempt to change attitudes. If acting out of self-interest is wrong for a politician, they reason such behavior on the part of a church must deserve just as much condemnation. Church congregations can always find high-minded arguments against recruiting new members, arguing that they could not possibly seek out people to join their church simply to get the bills paid. Some church members even object to recruiting others for the sake of the congregation's survival.

If they are theologically sophisticated, Christians can justify this utter disregard for their own collective interest by insisting that in being faithful to its crucified Lord the church must always be willing to die. Books like *A Theology of the Laity* by Hendrik Kraemer, a Dutch theologian, may allow us to conclude that the proper role of the church is to die. Kraemer does not actually say so, but he does maintain that the church is always provisional: "it exists on behalf of the world and not of itself."[1] Using these arguments, devoted followers of Jesus could easily conclude that if the church truly imitates Jesus, it also must die on behalf of the world, so that faithful congregations and even entire denominations would disappear.[2]

Practical Advantages to Church Growth

For congregations of any size to grow, the promise of life must be stronger than the appeal of death. The author of the Gospel according to St. John not only understood the promise of life but also saw a connection between abundant life and adding strangers to the group:

> The thief comes only to steal and kill and destroy. I came that they may have life, and have it abundantly....I am the good shepherd. I know my own and my own know me, just as the Father knows me and I know the Father. And I lay down my life for the sheep. I have other sheep that do not belong to this fold. I must bring them also, and they will listen to my voice. So there will be one flock, one shepherd. (John 10:10, 14-16)

Although the words may not originally have been intended for a congregation that seems determined to shrivel away, the imagery is apt. In the passage, those opposed to the work of Jesus promote death and destruction, while those who follow Jesus look for abundant life. They will not allow themselves to be scattered, but instead will be constantly on the lookout for others who do not belong to the group yet are willing to listen. Those who see congregational attitudes reflected in these words attributed to Jesus may see that they cannot separate having life abundantly from bringing in others who do not currently belong.

People who look for the abundant life exert a powerful influence over those around them. One such person, Bruce Sladen, was largely responsible for the survival of the congregation I now serve. Back in the early 1950s, when the church had dwindled to a few members and was without an ordained minister, the bishop suggested to the congregation that they find an elderly clergyman and close the church when he retired, advice in keeping with church trends in the neighborhood. Subsequently, the Lutheran and the Congregational churches closed their doors. In order to survive, the Presbyterians combined two congregations and the Methodists merged four churches into one. The Baptist church is now a condominium apartment building. In spite of its logic, however, Bruce Sladen objected to the bishop's counsel: "I didn't go through World War II, getting shot at and watching my buddies die, just to come home and lose my church." He convinced the other members that the church could live, and they found an ordained minister who would work with them to revitalize their congregation. With Bruce's active support, the church came to be a lively place that attracted people from all over the neighborhood, the city, and the suburbs.

Church members who prefer life to death understand that growing congregations have a vitality that can energize the lives of those who participate, while churches with a stable or declining membership can easily become dreary places that have a depressing effect on the people who belong to them. For church participation to be an uplifting experience, an openness to new members appears to be a requirement. Congregations that have no interest in attracting new members have a subtle attitude of rejection that permeates the atmosphere, making everyone feel a little less enthusiastic about life. They must discover at the personal as well as the institutional level the promise of new life in order to be open to a growth in membership. An increase in membership can produce new vitality for individuals as well as for the congregation in a variety of ways.

One positive aspect of having more people around is so obvious that church members can easily overlook it. A steady influx of new members will increase the possibility of finding people whose company they might enjoy. How many people complain about having too many friends? Many couples as well as single people living in large cities feel isolated and lonely, so they often join churches to make contacts with other people. Once they feel that they have been accepted and truly belong, they may think that they have all the human interaction they need. Then they find that good friends move away, or die, or become predictable and boring. Even in the company of other church members they experience their old feelings of isolation and loneliness. They are no longer particularly close to anyone in the congregation. With some, they have unresolved conflicts that do not seem worth the effort it would take to find a resolution; with others, they do not have enough in common to make the idea of dinner and an evening together seem at all attractive. New people present new possibilities for stimulating conversation and enjoyable companionship.

Stimulating conversation can produce new vitality in the congregation and in people's personal lives. People with no history in the congregation, or even in the wider church, have a fresh approach to every area of activity. In discussion with members who have been around for a while, new people may ask questions: Why doesn't the church have a hiking and camping group that could include single people as well as families? Why doesn't the church have a group to study the resurrection passages in the Bible, since they seem to bother so many of us? Why doesn't the church pay more attention to the problem of hunger in the world? Why don't we celebrate all twelve days of Christmas and end with a Feast of Fools on Twelfth Night? The answer to every one of these questions asked by new members is the same. Either nobody thought of it, or if somebody did have the idea, that person was afraid to bring it up for fear of being saddled with responsibility for the project. New people not only bring new ideas, they also frequently bring the time and energy to put their ideas into effect.

Ideas and energy are priceless resources for any congregation, but the money new people contribute also adds to the possibilities of the congregation offering better compensation to its staff as well as an expansion of services for the poor and the oppressed. Congregations with a stable or declining membership often become increasingly parsimonious. Fearful about the future, they try to protect their financial resources. An increase in available funds often helps to produce a more generous attitude that has a discernible ripple effect. With more money to spend, a congregation may take pride in paying its staff more adequate wages and in being more responsible about benefits like health insurance and pensions, especially for its lay employees. The pride a congregation takes in treating its staff well can boost morale throughout the membership. In a similar fashion, church members take more pride in their church when they know that the congregation is using some of its resources in an attempt to relieve suffering somewhere in the world outside of the church itself. The influx of funds provided by new people can generate both the pride that develops from taking better care of church workers and the pride that grows out of genuine service. This newly gained self-esteem will often produce an increase in parish vitality.

Perhaps the most important impact of increased church membership is an infusion of hope. A growing congregation has an optimistic attitude toward the future. When the members do not worry about their survival and do not try to protect themselves from the world around them, they look to the future with confidence. That hopeful attitude influences every discussion, decision, and action in the congregation. St. Paul ranked hope with faith and love, but hope is hard to find in many congregations. When hope is scarce or missing in a congregation, the members are not likely to come away from church with a hopeful attitude about their own situations, but the reverse is also true. When a congregation in its worship and activities sees the door to its future standing wide open, the members will find the hope they need to approach their individual futures with confidence.

If they can see something promising for themselves that might result from a growth in membership, members of a congregation will then be in a position to consider an even more threatening possibility: What might happen to them if they decided to welcome a different kind of person into their midst? Can they see anything promising about trying to absorb people whose beliefs differ markedly from their own or who have trouble believing at all?

Welcoming People with Doubts

Perhaps some Christians would consider the possibility a mixed blessing at best, but another benefit of welcoming into the congregation people who are openly skeptical about church doctrines is the affirmation that many of the existing members will experience. By accepting people who are outspoken about their doubts, the church will be compelled to deal openly with the subject of doubt. In the process, the partial skeptics and the secret skeptics who are already members of the church may find affirmation for themselves. All too often, the church members who have repressed their doubts live with a sense of shame, always thinking that they are not acceptable to God or to their fellow members. But once the church starts talking openly about doubt, everyone may discover that even the authors of the gospels expected doubting to be a characteristic of practicing Christians. Each offers a special understanding of doubt, and each conveys an appreciation of doubt held by the earliest followers of Jesus.

One story about doubt appears in an incident that Matthew sets in the last days of Jesus's life. Early in the morning, the day after Jesus had created a disturbance in the Temple by overturning the tables of the money changers, he and his disciples were walking back to Jerusalem from Bethany, where they had spent the night. Apparently they had departed without having eaten breakfast; Jesus was hungry. Having spotted a fig tree alongside the road, Jesus paused to look for fruit. When he found none, he cursed the fig tree, and it withered at once.

> When the disciples saw it, they were amazed, saying, "How did the fig tree wither at once?" Jesus answered them, "Truly I tell you, if you have faith and do not *doubt*, not only will you do what has been done to the fig tree, but even if you say to this mountain, 'Be lifted up and thrown into the sea,' it will be done." (Matthew 21:20-21)

The word translated as "doubt" is *diakrino,* meaning to discriminate or to judge.

If we can put aside for the moment any questions about the historical accuracy of the account, we can ask ourselves what the passage reveals about Matthew's attitude toward doubting. Are we to suppose that he had ever seen anyone curse a fig tree and cause it to wither at once, or even a week or two later? Are we to assume that he had watched while a mountain, following orders issued by a disciple of Jesus, rose up and crashed into the sea? Most of us will come to the conclusion that the answer to both questions is no—fig trees do not wither at unkind words and mountains have never been known to do what they are told, even by the most devout Christians. So what does Matthew mean when he has Jesus speak of such outrageously impossible events?

If their readers were to make sense of the Jesus story and the teachings of Jesus, the authors of the gospels had to assume they would understand Jesus's refusal to do magic tricks; he would not make stones into bread or show that he could jump unharmed from a temple pinnacle. The gospel writers also had to assume that their readers could discriminate between words that are to be taken at face value and words that fall into the category of hyperbole, exaggerations used for effect. The first readers must have been able to separate accurate descriptions from metaphors and to judge for themselves which passages were literary devices and which the authors intended to be taken more seriously.

It seems to me that the author of this passage in Matthew may have considered doubting a virtue necessary for understanding the gospel. The purpose of the passage may be to point out the absurdity of a certain magical view of religion. By employing hyperbole, metaphor, and the literary device of saying the opposite of what is meant, the storyteller lets the reader know that the followers of Jesus are discriminating—doubting—people who do not waste their time telling mountains or trees what to do.

In another story, Matthew has Jesus walking across the Sea of Galilee in a storm to join his disciples, who had gone ahead of him in a boat. When Peter decided he was seeing Jesus and not a ghost, he asked Jesus to command him to come across on the water.

> He said, "Come." So Peter got out of the boat, started walking on the water, and came toward Jesus. But when he noticed the strong wind, he became frightened, and beginning to sink, he cried out, "Lord, save me!" Jesus immediately reached out his hand and caught him, saying to him, "You of little faith, why did you *doubt?*" (Matthew 14:29-31)

The word here for "doubt" is *distazo,* meaning to waver or to hesitate.

The questions in the Bible are always worth pondering, especially in a case like this where no answer follows. Sometimes we are tempted to skip over the questions because they do not seem to be genuine questions but rather appear to be reprimands. In our ways of speaking to one another today, we seldom begin a question with "why" when we are expecting information. When a mother says to her son, "Why didn't you wash your hands before coming to the table?" she is not asking for an explanation but telling him that he was wrong in coming to supper with dirty hands and that he better hurry to the bathroom and correct the situation. Perhaps that is the way Matthew intends the reader to hear Jesus's question to Peter, simply as a rebuke. But even if we do not hear the question as a reprimand, we might still ignore the question because it sounds so silly. Why wouldn't Peter waver or hesitate in an attempt to walk on water, and why wouldn't any sane person think at least twice before getting out of the boat?

In spite of the possibility that we may be dealing with a rebuke or a silly question, I think the author may have been using the story to pose a serious question about the purpose of doubting. When a person faces an entirely new set of circumstances entailing both predictable and unknown risks, what value can be found in wavering, or having second thoughts? Although sometimes hesitating betrays weakness or cowardice, rash or impetuous action can get a person into a trouble. Think of a young couple buying a house for the first time. If on their first day of looking they find what seems to be their dream house, should they immediately sign a contract and write a check for a deposit, or should they keep looking to assure themselves that they are making a sound choice? If they delay, someone else may put in a contract on the house, and they may never find anything else that they like nearly so well. If they act immediately, they may discover later that they paid too much or that the dining room is really too small or that the neighborhood has few young families.

Matthew may well have been using the question about Peter's hesitation to make the reader think about the function of doubt in facing any decision, but he may have been particularly concerned with decisions about religious dedication. We are always surrounded by religious leaders who promise salvation in exchange for our complete loyalty. Before pledging fidelity to one of them, we would do well to hesitate, to think twice about what we are doing. Doubting can be our protection against making quick and foolish decisions, especially when some person or institution is trying to extract a commitment from us. By raising the issue of doubt in a dramatic story about Peter, Matthew invites the reader to pause and ponder how doubt may work among the loyal followers of Jesus.

It is important to remember that encounters with God almost always include elements of fear and doubt. In Luke's account of what happened to the disciples after Jesus died, the disciples are left on their own in Jerusalem, wondering what to do next. On the third day after the crucifixion, they hear that Jesus has appeared to Peter. Then two other followers of Jesus report an appearance of Jesus to them in Emmaus, and that same evening Jesus appears to all the disciples.

> While they were talking about this, Jesus himself stood among them and said to them, "Peace be with you." They were startled and terrified, and thought that they were seeing a ghost. He said to them,

"Why are you frightened, and why do *doubts* arise in your hearts?"
(Luke 24:36-38)

Here the word for "doubts" is the Greek noun *dialogismos*. As you
probably can guess from the English word that evolved from it, *dialogismos* meant discussion, debate, or thought. In this case the dialogue is internal, in the hearts of the disciples. Jesus assumes that
each disciple is having a discussion within himself in response to the
sudden appearance of Jesus. The disciples are startled and terrified,
but by his question Jesus implies that they are still able to think.
Whether Luke meant to suggest that thinking for themselves was an
admirable or reprehensible thing for the disciples to be doing, no
one can say for certain. This passage presents the same sort of difficulty that we encountered in Jesus's words to Peter when he attempted to walk on water; it may be intended as a rebuke, or Luke
might mean something else. Who would not be terrified if a dead
friend appeared out of nowhere? In my opinion, however, all of the
unanswerable questions in the Bible are a deliberate attempt on the
part of the authors to lead the readers more deeply into an awareness of the mystery we call God.

Why are you afraid, and why do you have a debate in your heart
when you perceive yourself to be in the presence of God? A young
architect told me that on the night before surgery to remove a lump
in her breast, when she was all alone in her hospital room, she felt
what seemed like God's presence. At first she was afraid; perhaps
she was about to die. She was also afraid of God's judgment; she was
not at all proud of some of things she had done to get ahead in her
profession. Then she started thinking and wondering if this was God
at all. Maybe she was just going through a psychological reaction to
the stress of surgery and the threat of cancer. Before she went to
sleep, however, she decided God was with her to uphold her and to
give her courage. She was no longer afraid. The experience has
stayed with her. In subsequent moments of crisis she has had occasion to think about the night before her surgery. She admits that
what she experienced may have been nothing more than a psychological phenomenon, but she prefers to think about what happened
as an encounter with God.

Although the gospels use different words for doubt, the writers use them all in a similar fashion. The people doing the doubting are in every case Jesus's closest friends. By contrast, the gospels never characterize those who oppose Jesus as doubters; the Pharisees, the Sadducees, and the Roman officials are sure of themselves and of their beliefs. They are not troubled by the necessity of making difficult distinctions; they do not waver or hesitate; they do not carry on debates in their hearts. The only people in the gospel stories who doubt are the disciples. In the gospels, to be a follower of Jesus is to be capable of doubt.

Whenever a congregation makes an effort to welcome openly doubting and questioning people, they not only serve the cause of evangelism but also give themselves the chance to take a fresh look at the gospel stories and gain a new appreciation for the function of doubt. Doubt keeps open the questions that draw people ever more deeply into the mystery of their own lives and of God. What they will find will be "gospel"—good news for all the seeking and uncertain ones in their midst. When they are no longer ashamed of their doubts, all the members of the church who harbor any degree of skepticism will feel that at last they really belong.

Challenge and Stimulation

These secret questioners are not the only members of a congregation who might profit from the arrival of openly skeptical people. People who ask questions and are vocal about their doubts can help keep all professed Christians in the congregation from allowing their sensitivities to become dull. To keep sharp, most people must subject themselves to some form of abrasive contact. Good athletes as well as professional singers need not only the stimulation of public performances but also the challenge of their coaches to keep their skills honed. Self-proclaimed skeptics can provide a similar kind of testing for people who have been in the church for a long time.

Most Christians like to think of themselves as unselfish people, generous with the time and money they are willing to spend on their church and on those in need. The real challenge may come when they are confronted with the possibility of being generous with their spiritual community. Their generosity will be tested every time a provocative question makes them uncomfortable, every time the worship planners make a change to accommodate the doubtful, every time they find strangers sitting in the places that they long ago began to think of as their own. If they respond positively to the tests, the church members will find that their capacity for unselfish action may expand.

Honesty is another virtue that can improve in response to uninvited questions. All of us have a well-developed faculty for self-deception, especially in matters related to faith. Certain troublesome areas we can leave perpetually unexamined. What do we mean when we say that Jesus is the Son of God? We can spend a lifetime in the church without thinking about the implications of such a question. Then we let in a skeptical sort of person who asks the question directly and who wants to know the implications. What kind of a claim about Jesus are Christians making? What does that claim say about other religions? What behavior is expected of a person who joins in making the claim? Under the pressure of such questions, church-goers may start getting honest with themselves about previously unexamined areas of their spiritual lives.

Both honesty and generosity come under challenge when the questions focus on the church's attitude toward the poor and oppressed. When people with a long history of skepticism about organized religion come into the church, they often want to know what the congregation is doing about hunger and poverty. In the years before they express interest in the church, many people find meaning in public service. Soon after graduating from college, Chuck, for example, had volunteered as a Big Brother for an inner-city child whose father had abandoned the family. Chuck had also spent vacations working with Habitat for Humanity to build houses for people who could not afford to pay market rates for decent housing. When he affiliated with a church, he began to ask whether his fellow parishioners were not more concerned about their own spiritual health than that of the larger community around them. People like Chuck have a way of pointing out incongruities between the church's professed values and the actual behavior of the congregation. If members of the church choose to respond by devoting more of their resources to the ill-fed and poorly sheltered, they may notice an increase in their ability to be both generous and honest.

The questioning of authority also can be a service to the church. Leaders need to be questioned, both to keep them from taking themselves too seriously and to prevent the members from taking them too seriously. Unquestioned religious authority leads to disasters like Waco, Texas, and Jonestown; on a less dramatic or tragic scale, it can lead to dependence and arrested religious development for the membership. People who are skeptical about the wisdom or good sense of church authorities can contribute a great deal to the health of the organization by asking embarrassing questions about either finances or theology. Who really makes the decisions about how the church spends money? What is this church doing to see that hungry people are fed? Why do you put so much emphasis on the Bible when it makes so little sense to the average person? Where in the Bible or the Christian tradition does it say that two people of the same sex are not supposed to set up housekeeping as a committed couple? The questions do not have to be hostile to be helpful. If the questions are genuine requests for information, they will probably provide the most useful challenge, the kind of testing that can help everyone in the church maintain a balanced view of authority.

Jim Kelley, a thoroughgoing skeptic, has served our congregation well by asking the same sort of probing questions that he had used in his capacity as an administrative law judge. As editor of the monthly parish newsletter, Jim kept the congregation abreast of any controversies that might otherwise have been kept out of sight. The voting members of the congregation developed such respect for his integrity that they elected him to our governing board, the vestry. While serving on the vestry, he continued to ask the embarrassing questions that had established his reputation. For example, he wanted to know what the church was actually paying for clergy. Our salaries in the budget seemed modest, to say the least, but he suspected that hidden in the numbers were benefits that are much more generous than those received by government employees or by people working in the private sector of the economy. He suggested that the mystery surrounding clergy compensation must have been intentional on someone's part, a way of increasing the likelihood of raises by making the congregation feel guilty for overworking and underpaying the ordained ministers. When all the relevant figures were assembled on one page, anyone could see that his suspicions had been well-founded. When the vestry added in the tax-free housing allowances, the premiums the church was paying in full for life and health insurance and for a pension plan, and the allowances for travel and for half the self-employment tax, they discovered that they were compensating their clergy at a respectable level. Clearing away the mystery with his pointed questions, Jim helped clear away misplaced guilt so that the vestry could deal with clergy compensation rationally and responsibly.

Religion, like science and democracy, thrives on challenges to authority. Little progress could be made in astronomy until Galileo challenged the authorities who held the view that the earth was the center of the universe. The citizens of the United States have the world's oldest and most stable government, over two hundred years with one constitution, because people like Samuel Adams and Thomas Jefferson were willing to challenge the authority of the British crown. Without skepticism, advances in science and in public policy would not be possible. In much the same fashion, no progress would be possible in religion without people like Jesus of Nazareth challenging the views held by those in authority. In many ways, skeptical people can do more for a congregation than the passively loyal members. Jesus may have had skeptical people in mind when he reportedly observed, "The children of this age are more shrewd in dealing with their own generation than are the children of light."

In recent years, researchers have been making a distinction between "extrinsic" and "intrinsic" religion. People with an extrinsic attitude toward religion tend to be dogmatic and prejudiced, expecting God to solve their problems or at least to make them feel better. They are looking for social or emotional results from their religion. When tested, they prove to have higher levels of anxiety and depression than people with an intrinsic view of religion. The latter kind do not approach God because they have a problem to solve, but because they want to be in communion with God. In the analysis of Richard Gorsuch, a psychologist at Fuller Theological Seminary, "Job's was an intrinsic religiosity, because he could still maintain communion with God even though everything had gone wrong."[3]

When skeptics discover the value of intrinsic religion, they can become invaluable members of congregations. They can remind people of the damage they can do to themselves in expecting God to provide more favorable circumstances for their lives or to make them feel more comfortable. They can encourage people to develop a more intrinsic attitude; that is, to develop a confidence in God that will sustain them in their discomfort. The contribution they make to the mental health of the church comes through their irreverent remarks and their open challenges when anyone suggests that God will set things right.

When a growing church has attracted a sufficient number of members whose religion is truly intrinsic, the congregation can afford to develop a warm welcome for those who are more fervent in their religion. Fervent Christians—from St. Francis to the couple just back from a Cursillo weekend—can be dependent and a bit unstable, but the enthusiasm they bring to their religion can energize parish life. While their belief that God is leading them may make them anxious with success and depressed by failure, their confidence can sometimes spark action from their more rational sisters and brothers in the congregation. If a small group honestly believes that God has called them to start a shelter for homeless men, they may be more likely to steer the congregation toward actual work on the project than a group working from a more analytical perspective. Still, without the balance to their fervor provided by those with an intrinsic orientation, the extrinsic ones can create problems for themselves and the congregation. In their single-minded effort to do God's will, they can neglect their businesses and families and evoke hostility from those who resent devoting so much of the parish's resources to one project. A congregation that can make room for both types may prove to be the most effective organization to serve the community around the church.

Hope for the Future

If members of a congregation striving to grow see some promise for themselves, both from increasing membership and from making skeptics welcome, they may find that the greatest possibility for the future comes from putting the two together. The best opportunities for growth can be found in opening the doors of the church to the skeptical, the dubious, and the agnostic.

The non-affiliated are not necessarily hostile to the idea of joining a church. In a survey of the unchurched, the Gallup Organization asked what circumstances could cause them to return to church. The most frequent response, that made by thirty-seven percent of those questioned, indicated that the person would go to a church "if I can find a pastor or priest with whom I can openly express my spiritual needs and religious doubts."[4] If those in the survey are representative of the general population outside of the church, many people would welcome the opportunity to explore their doubts but would have no interest in accepting dogma. They would feel at home in a church that understood doubting as a virtue to be expected of practicing Christians.

What would most encourage people to try out a church happens to be what another survey shows would keep them there. A study of ten thousand Protestants that focused on the question of what matters most in developing an integrated faith came to this conclusion:

> Growth in mature faith depended not so much on the warmth and friendliness of the congregation, but on the degree to which it challenges thinking and encourages questions about values, theology, politics and scripture.[5]

With its emphasis on having the right answers, conventional evangelism discourages thinking and questioning, but an evangelism designed to meet the needs of those with a skeptical mind-set can both attract and hold the interest of people who would not come close to a dogmatic church.

Perhaps questioning people have not always been open to what the church has to offer. During the 1980s, the decade of greed, the interest level may not have been what it has proved to be more recently. The change in attitudes appears to have coincided with the transition from one decade to the next. In one of its first issues of the new decade, *Fortune* magazine included religion in a survey of "What Consumers Want in the 1990s." The article proclaimed the "end of the myth of Me" and went on to declare that narcissism is out and so is dog-eat-dog ambition. The business-oriented publication prophesied that in this decade "Americans will seek a sense of moral stability."[6] That prediction seems to be holding true. Churches that stress behavior instead of belief are in a position to make welcome the people who want to develop moral values and who want to find meaning by serving people other than themselves.

That a church could grow by appealing to thinking people, instead of relying on conventional evangelism, is not just a theory. All Saints' Episcopal Church in downtown Pasadena, California, has grown to three thousand members by offering intellectually stimulating sermons and forums and by emphasizing issues of peace and justice. A Baptist church in the San Fernando Valley grew rapidly after it dropped the Baptist label and style. A parishioner described what he and his family liked about the congregation, now called Shepherd of the Hills: "There's a spirit of putting people over doctrine and denominations. The attitude is that they are for life, love and liberty—it's more *for* things than *against* things."[7] These two congregations that have gained national recognition are by no means the only churches that have grown by deemphasizing doctrine so that people are free to discover God's presence. On the opposite coast, St. Columba's became the largest Episcopal church in Washington, D.C., while encouraging people to think for themselves. The Unitarian-Universalist Church, with its long tradition of accepting agnostics, continues to grow. My own congregation, which surprised most observers by not only surviving but also flourishing in the shadow of the nation's Capitol, began its road to recovery by putting under the windshield wipers of neighborhood cars handbills addressed to "Interested Pagans, Bored Christians, Others."

After a careful consideration of the promises attached to a strategy of growth based on an appeal to questioning people, a congregation needs to weigh the costs before plunging ahead. The costs will be substantial. Loss and pain will accompany a change of direction. Although I obviously think no price is too high for opening up the church to people who have difficulty believing, other church people can responsibly reach the opposite conclusion.

Chapter 4

The Costs of
Evangelism

A few years ago some members of our congregation organized a group to read and discuss Thomas Sheehan's *The First Coming: How the Kingdom of God Became Christianity.* Most of them found the book helped them with the problems they had with traditional explanations of what happened to Jesus after his death. It gave them permission to claim the Christian faith without necessarily subscribing to the proposition that Jesus literally got up out of his tomb.

Not everyone who heard about the book agreed with its conclusions, however. The idea that the resurrection was not an event, but the interpretation of an event, so bothered one member of the congregation, Robert Headley, Jr., that he sent a protest to our parish newsletter. "Some of us find Thomas Sheehan's interpretation of the resurrection shocking," he wrote. "I personally find it breathtakingly bankrupt." Headley complained that the book took one of the most wonderful events in history and trivialized it to the point of absurdity. How could a despondent group of people reduced to hiding behind closed doors have been inspired by some intellectual realization or insight—no matter how profound—to leave their hiding places and go boldly into a hostile world to preach the gospel? "It all comes down to this for me," he concluded. "If there was no resurrection—and I mean a real resurrection of the dead—I don't want to have anything to do with Christianity. If Christ didn't die on the cross and rise from the dead, for me, there can be nothing wonderful after the crucifixion. I can't worship an insight or a profound realization."

Headley's words point up one of the very real costs of evangelism, a cost that is particularly high for those intelligent and active Christians who hold dear the traditional doctrines of the church. The more skeptical members of the congregation could not dismiss his remarks by caricaturing his views as those of an uneducated and uninformed man, since he is a university professor who typifies those intelligent and active traditional believers. Such people are honor-bound to object when the church eagerly welcomes anyone who does not profess the beliefs that they hold as central to the Christian faith.

Other members of the church, who may or may not care much about doctrines and beliefs, are going to be upset simply at the thought of adding to their numbers. The major price a congregation will pay for trying to engage in any attempt to increase membership will surface almost immediately. Members will make their displeasure known in a variety of ways: less frequent attendance at worship, reduction in financial support, or more vocal complaints. If the leadership of the church persists in an effort to attract new people, they will have to deal with the negative attitudes of many present members or else allow them to sabotage the program. Many clergy prefer to avoid open conflict, but avoidance of resistance to evangelism may doom the program to defeat. The unhappy members, consciously or unconsciously, will poison the atmosphere with their negativity, making sure that visitors will be unlikely to return. For new people to feel welcome, the whole congregation must convey a receptive attitude. To have any chance at all of gaining the congregation's support, those who favor making the church a more accepting place may have to spend a considerable amount of time and effort with the resistant parishioners.

Identifying Fears

Part of the strategy in handling the people who do not want their church to grow must be spending time to listen to them and to help them identify their fears. Identification of fears can take place in parish meetings and adult forums, but the elected leaders and the clergy may have to concentrate on listening in their private conversations with influential people who are obviously upset. Many of them will not understand their negativity until they can name what frightens them about the idea of expanding the membership. When they come to recognize the basis of their fears, they may or may not become more open.

Often people are afraid that an increase in membership will cause them to lose their sense of belonging. They may already have experienced some feeling of loss in recent years just through the normal turnover in membership: "I used to know everybody in the church, but last Sunday I looked around and hardly saw a face I recognized." Behind the expression of dismay at not knowing the other people assembled for worship lies the unspoken fear of not being known. At a still deeper level, the fear of not being known may awaken the primitive terror of utter isolation that will become absolute in death. Perhaps it sounds absurd to suggest that parishioners may resist the active recruitment of new members because they fear death, but I think the intensity of the resistance indicates the presence of a primary fear.

A member of one congregation, in objecting to a more active attempt to recruit new members, hinted at another basic fear by comparing the life of the parish to a pot of soup. His mother had told him that during the Depression, when his family was extremely poor, if company came to call and stayed for supper his grandmother simply added more water to the soup. The more people who came to the table, the less nourishment each received. He felt that for years he had found nourishment through his participation in the life of the church, but if too many others showed up, each person's experience would be diluted. Eventually no one would be given enough to eat.

Another parishioner, who had been listening to the "watered soup" analogy, countered that what would be diluted would not be spiritual nourishment but power. He had a good point. In a small congregation, even people who are not in direct control of the parish's business can exercise considerable influence through their friends. Any increase in membership reduces each person's share of power. The loss of power over the affairs of the church would be felt acutely by those people who feel powerless in other areas of their lives—who feel their lives are controlled by their employers, by the insurance companies, by Congress and the legislature, by the Internal Revenue Service, and by the drug gangs who seem to own the streets after dark. If church is the only place where you feel you have some control over what happens, an increase in membership is indeed like watering the soup.

Closely allied to the fear of shrinking power is the fear of a loss of status. Working at the office or going about the daily routine in the city, a person may feel like a nobody, but church is different. At church a person may be somebody, somebody with a title: deacon or elder, chairman or warden, superintendent or director. He or she might represent the congregation at a meeting of the presbytery, or synod, or convention. Even people who do not currently hold an office that carries a title can walk into church with a certain confidence, knowing that people will remember their years of active service. But new people will have no way of remembering. They will not pay attention or give deference. A person may still belong but may no longer have the opportunity to feel special if too many new people join the congregation. We should not underestimate the importance of status on a person's sense of well-being; without it, he or she becomes disoriented. Many hope that by resisting an influx of new members in the church, they might avoid an unpleasant episode of disorientation.

One way to help parishioners deal with the fears associated with losing their place in the church is to invite them to a deeper level of faith. By listening to sermons on the subject and by participating in adult education groups, they may discover that they have been using the church as the answer to their fears of isolation and of being of no account. If so, the church has become a substitute for God, rather than an arena in which the presence of God is recognized and celebrated. They might come to see that the Spirit's capacity to nourish is unlimited, that being part of the company of all faithful people provides all the belonging they will ever need, that being a child of God confers all the status anyone might require.

Such a process of faith development will demand a great deal of those who lead as well as those who are asked to participate. The desire for a clear sense of place is so great that most people who attempt to lead others in strengthening their faith easily fall prey to the temptation of ranking people according to a scale based on the experience of the leaders. In some congregations members win recognition by chairing committees, in others by attending retreats, in others by gaining skills as group facilitators or as teachers. As a consequence, the leaders may skew the process by simply replicating the old system of belonging and status in a new form. The demand on the participants, even with the best of leaders, is also formidable. They are invited to let go of the place that has sustained them without any guarantee that they will have a deeper awareness of God.

Some people can feel settled and comfortable with their faith until they find themselves confronted by outsiders with new questions and different attitudes. When they cannot provide satisfactory answers to the questions that more skeptical people ask, they become anxious, unsure of their faith. A widow in her late sixties complained that she never questioned her religion—she simply believed what she had been taught as a child—until she found herself in a Bible class with a number of skeptics. As they asked questions that pointed up the contradictions and improbabilities in the Bible passages, she began to wonder what was really true and what she really did believe. The experience was too much for her. She dropped out of the class, explaining that at her time of life she didn't want her faith shaken but strengthened. Other members of the class, including the leader and two women of her own age, went to see her with the intention of convincing her to come back to the class. Although she was gracious in her refusal to return and seemed to appreciate the attention, she left the rest of the class to struggle with their feelings of failure and to wonder how they might better have acknowledged her faith.

Many church members deal with their doubts by repressing or ignoring them. These are the secret skeptics who have kept their doubts a secret even from themselves, sometimes going on for years acting as if they were believers. They might even keep up the pretense until the day they die, if no one challenges them. Once challenged, those who cannot accept the truth about themselves and their doubts may become vociferous in their defense of orthodoxy and put themselves out of harm's way by joining a Roman Catholic or a fundamentalist church. The ones who can accept the truth about their doubting natures may also leave—not to join another church but to disappear from church altogether. After uncovering their doubts, they begin to feel a sense of remorse for their long-term charade. They avoid church so that they will not be reminded of their years of hypocrisy and intellectual dishonesty.

The loss of once-faithful members to conservative churches or to secularism probably will alarm the clergy·and those parishioners who want their congregation to grow. The leadership will become even more alarmed when they discover that every change they make to broaden the congregation's appeal may create enough upset to cause an exodus of their present members. It seems self-defeating to drive some people out of the church in order to accommodate others, who may or may not show up in sufficient numbers to replace the ones who have been lost. If a congregation gets to this point, it will be an anxious time.

In looking back over the records of the congregation I serve, I discovered that the attendance and membership figures did not show a consistent pattern of growth starting with the decision to welcome people with a variety of beliefs. For several years the church actually continued to decline in numbers as the energy and enthusiasm for new life developed. With every change made to accommodate people who had been alienated from the church, some of the old members left in protest. The first time some new members presented a play in the chancel, for example, people left. The first time beer was served in the parish hall, others left. When the art class engaged the services of a woman to pose in the nude, a few protested to the bishop that "there must be some canon law that forbids naked ladies in the church," but most of the offended people simply left.

For others, the loss of the church pews was the final blow. A year-long study of architecture and theology had convinced the new leadership that a central altar table would better represent their current point of view than continued use of the old stone altar against the far wall of the chancel. When the old members came to church one Sunday and discovered that during the week the rector had sold the pews, they were horrified and never came back. Those were anxious times.

If a church tries to incorporate new members who have had problems with organized religion, it must face the possibility that it might get smaller before it starts to grow. If the sermons become more open-ended and less reassuring, some people will leave. If the clergy spend more time on adult education and less time with existing organizations, others may feel neglected and withdraw. If the worship becomes more relaxed, some will become upset and start looking for a church in which the liturgy is more dignified. The fear that the church may lose members is as realistic as the fear that the church might grow.

Careful Use of Religious Language

An intelligent approach to evangelism will place great demands on the church members who decide to stay. They will not only have to deal with their doubts and adjust to new ways of doing things, they also will have to develop new ways of talking about their faith in order to communicate clearly when engaged in discussion with people who have become thoroughly secularized. To complicate their lives further, they will also have to learn how to translate secular expressions into their theological equivalents.

Church people often develop a habit of tossing out pious comments without stopping to think about what the words mean or how they will sound in the ears of an outsider. Take as an example the church member who describes the plight of a friend recently audited by the Internal Revenue Service and charged several thousand dollars in back taxes and accumulated interest. He concludes his narrative with a familiar comment, "There but for the grace of God go I." Other church people know what he means—he is thankful that he has never been audited and forced to pay back taxes, and he realizes the IRS auditors' failure to pay him a visit is just a matter of luck. He means that whenever he feels thankful and fortunate, his thoughts turn to God. What the person unaccustomed to church talk hears might be something different—that God plays favorites. God allows one man to make mistakes or to claim undeserved deductions and then arranges for him to be caught and punished, but prevents the prying eyes of the IRS auditors from seeing similar problems in the tax returns of the speaker. In short, the secular person may hear what sounds like a totally unacceptable theological position: God intervenes in history arbitrarily to favor some people while allowing others to suffer.

The theology implied by "There but for the grace of God go I" becomes particularly offensive when used in reference to being spared from disability or death. A Jewish survivor of Hitler's holocaust has offended more people than he will ever know by attributing his survival to the grace of God and by becoming a Christian out of gratitude. Jews are not alone in abhorring the thought that God decided to save the survivor, allowing him to ponder his miraculous deliverance while he stacked "like wooden boards" the bodies of those whose plight God chose to ignore.[1]

Once church members become sensitive to the misunderstandings that can arise through the casual use of a theological word such as "grace," they may feel compelled to take a fresh look at the way the term appears in the Bible. If they take the trouble to make such a study, they will discover that by the grace of God people receive justification, righteousness, and salvation—but never relief from difficult circumstances. By grace people experience repentance, forgiveness, and faith—but not food, money, or employment. By grace they discover their own capacities, abilities, and ministries—but they are not healed of diseases. In the Bible, grace is not a matter of luck nor of God playing favorites. Although the word itself may once have meant an act of kindness given without obligation, the way the followers of Jesus used the word it always included a sense of individual responsibility that God's benevolence had evoked. If practicing Christians are going to use the word grace in their conversations with skeptical people, they will have to find a manner of speaking that is both understandable and theologically defensible.

Norman Maclean, known best for his book that became a motion picture with the same title, *A River Runs Through It,* understood the biblical meaning of grace and wrote about grace in a way that both the secular person and the practicing Christian can understand. Maclean spent much of his time during his last years coming to terms with his wife's death from cancer as he tried to find out how twelve smoke jumpers came to die in a Montana forest fire thirty years earlier:

> At times it seems as if tragedy tries at the end to take away some of
> its own tragedy, and if some tragedies never restore our stability, at
> least most of them allow us some success in struggling to attain some
> stability of our own. In my family, some such meaning was attached
> to the phrase "saved by grace."...In my family, what happens on
> Sundays is foreordained. What comes on weekdays comes from

within us and for which we are responsible, and if it comes from deep within us it is called "grace," and it is.[2]

Church members who want to communicate with outsiders are obliged to adopt a disciplined use of religious language, finding ordinary words that can be used as substitutes or that can clarify what they mean. For example, look at the titles Christians attach to the name of Jesus: Lord, Savior, Christ. The words may slip easily off the tongue of someone familiar with Christian worship, but without careful thought they may have little meaning for the person who uses them and a decidedly negative impact on the hearer. With some study and thought, however, church people can find ways to use these titles in communicating what matters to them. "Lord" can be a reminder that any group is inseparable from some symbolic expression that gives the association shape and direction. From street gangs to garden clubs, those who belong have learned what kind of behavior the group requires; people have agreed to give allegiance to some law-giver, which may be an ideal or an actual person. Frequently the lord is also a "savior," but to use this second title meaningfully, the speaker will need to be clear about what a person might want to be saved from. The title suggests finding help in a time of extremity, such as the grip of anxiety or the depths of despair.

Even the title "Christ" must be given a context; it is not enough to say that Christ means "messiah" or "the anointed one." What do Jesus's followers mean when they say that he is Christ for them? In the gospel stories, people who call Jesus their christ are those who receive a way of facing the truth about themselves and of finding a new way of life. The fourth chapter of John's gospel tells the story of such a person, a woman whom Jesus met at a well in Samaria. Her encounter with Jesus, far from burdening her with the guilt and dismay of her past life, filled her with a sense of enthusiasm about what might lie ahead. With similar stories and with plain language, Christians can find the way to communicate with outsiders, but they cannot avoid the effort that such conversation requires.

At the same time that practicing Christians must be careful about their use of theological language around people to whom it is unfamiliar, they must learn to translate the secular language they hear into familiar religious idioms if they hope to find common ground with those they are trying to make welcome in the church. For example, Cathleen Schine—who was a guest contributor to the "On Language" column in the *New York Times Magazine*—has perceptively discovered the reason for the rapidly spreading use of the adverb "hopefully" at the beginning or the end of a sentence, as in, "Hopefully, I will survive this operation." Although the use of an adverb without a verb or adjective for it to modify violates a basic rule of grammar, the word's acceptance by the public demonstrates that it has filled a gap in the language for people who think they are not religious.

> *Hopefully* means "God willing" in a secular world. *Hopefully* means: I don't know if there is a God, I don't know if the world makes sense, I don't know if there is meaning or order or heaven or hell, but please let everything turn out O.K. It is a prayer to no one, a plea for help from an individual to he knows not what, a shout of confidence in one's existence (I'm here! Whether you are or not!), a tender call for understanding, a cry of love for love.[3]

Listening for the religious meaning hidden in secular language requires both concentration and an earnest desire to find what longings and fears people have in common. Practicing Christians will have an opportunity to connect with skeptical people if they listen for hints of what they are seeking and of what disturbs them. When the conversation strays into areas of belief, divisions rather than connections will be most apparent. Giving up talk of belief to maintain a connection with a skeptical person can be very difficult for a person whose beliefs have proved valuable in keeping a sense of equilibrium. Letting the longings and fears get too close to the surface of consciousness can be destabilizing. People who want their experience of church to produce an outward calm and an inner peace may not be willing to put themselves in a position where they could easily be upset in a conversation with an unbeliever.

Surrendering Faith and Beliefs

This careful use of language in evangelism demands more of the practicing Christian than a willingness to engage in an intellectual exercise. The willingness to speak and listen carefully will inevitably lead to a renewed awareness of unresolved fears and unfulfilled longings. When these fears and longings are no longer held in check by talk about beliefs or faith, church members may feel that they have given up too much for the sake of making outsiders feel welcome. If Jack has kept a fear of dying in check by a firm belief in life after death, and if he longs to be reunited with his parents in heaven, he is going to have a hard time talking about death with an outsider who thinks that any sort of life beyond the grave is superstitious nonsense. To engage the outsider in genuine conversation, Jack will have to show respect for the other person's position by entertaining the possibility that he could be wrong and that death means oblivion. Even allowing himself to imagine briefly that death could mean oblivion could stir up his fear and grief. Perhaps no one should ask such sacrifices of a church member, but before a congregation decides the price is too high, it might consider the instructions St. Paul wrote to the Christian community at Philippi:

> Let the same mind be in you that was in Christ Jesus, who, though he was in the form of God, did not regard equality with God as something to be exploited, but emptied himself, taking the form of a slave, being born in human likeness. And being found in human form, he humbled himself and became obedient to the point of death—even death on a cross. (Philippians 2:5-8)

Jesus emptied himself—of what? The followers of Jesus are to be of the same mind, to empty themselves, but of what? Jesus took the likeness and form of human beings. What likeness and form are the followers of Jesus to take? I find the poetic advice of St. Paul to be wonderfully ambiguous, but I cannot help thinking that perhaps what he had in mind was something like this. To make a connection with ordinary human beings, Jesus emptied himself of his extraordinary confidence and trust. If we are to have the same mind, we will be willing to empty ourselves of faith and belief to make a connection with people who do not use the language of faith and who do not have beliefs at all similar to ours. For Jesus, the experience was like that of becoming a slave, giving up control over the circumstances of his life, even to the point of dying an untimely death. All people who empty themselves of faith and belief for the sake of other people will have an experience that is something like becoming a slave and dying. It will mean loss of control and loss of security, an increase in anxiety and anguish. If that was what he meant, perhaps Paul was expecting too much of the Philippian Christians. Perhaps people should never be asked to empty themselves for the sake of others, but we have been asked. Now each congregation and each individual Christian has to answer.

If church members try to figure out what emptying themselves might mean, they might see that becoming absorbed in their quest for individual salvation could be at odds with what Jesus had in mind for his followers. What some Christians mean by "faith" suggests that their desire for inner peace matters more than their responsibility to make the way of Jesus open to people who are unable to have beliefs like theirs. I have a hard time trying to imagine that Jesus was putting forward such a self-centered approach to life, but perhaps the only way that some people can function at all is to put their faith first in their lists of priorities. Maybe the letter to the Ephesians was correct in assuming that not everyone is called to be an evangelist. "The gifts he gave were that *some* would be...evangelists."

Evangelism and Bible Study

Part of the cost of evangelism is the difficulty of finding a new way to approach the Bible and Christian tradition for those to whom these are foreign or off-putting. For those willing to be evangelists, often the most difficult area is the traditional conviction that at a particular moment in history at a particular place—just outside the Jerusalem city wall—Jesus of Nazareth, who had been crucified, was raised from the dead and brought out of the tomb in which he had been buried. Belief in the resurrection of Jesus as an historical event constitutes the foundation on which the Christian faith is built. Unless Christians demand from all new members a belief in the historicity of Jesus's resurrection, the Christian faith will lose its integrity. To demand less in the way of believing simply to accommodate people of an analytical frame of mind would be like adding water to fine wine to make it more palatable to children.

Convinced Christians, eloquent in the defense of their faith, find themselves in a difficult position when they are asked, for the sake of evangelism, to make room in their churches for those for whom belief in the resurrection is a stumbling-block. If they insist that everyone must accept a literal resurrection from the dead, they close the door to people who simply cannot accept as fact what cannot be verified. If they throw open the door, they betray their convictions. How can someone whose faith depends on a real resurrection live faithfully with this dilemma?

In trying to include doubters in the conversation about resurrection, convinced Christians do not have to agree with the insights of biblical criticism to use the tools the scholars have provided for the sake of evangelism. It is useful to remember, for example, that no follower of Jesus was actually a witness to the resurrection. In the Bible, the only possible witnesses were the guards, who appear in Matthew's version of the events. Although they became like "dead men" when the angel appeared, they were able to tell the chief priests "everything that had happened." The chief priests apparently believed the report of the guards, but in spite of knowing that Jesus was raised from the dead, as far as we know neither the guards nor the chief priests chose to become Jesus followers. *The Gospel according to St. Peter,* which did not make its way into the Bible, elaborates on the story and includes Jewish elders as actual witnesses to the coming of the angels and the raising of Jesus, but none of those who see Jesus being raised believe in him. As Thomas Sheehan puts it, "If one does not have faith already, neither the pronouncements of angels nor the emptiness of tombs can provide it."[4] People who have faith in the emptiness of the tomb and the pronouncement of the angels can testify to the centrality of the resurrection in their beliefs and can allow a place in the church for other faithful people who may not have placed much confidence in the details associated with the event. They can hold to their position while helping the dubious find meaning in the resurrection accounts.

To help adult inquirers come to terms with the resurrection takes time and effort. In my experience, the best approach is to organize groups willing to wrestle with the doctrine of the resurrection. The enterprise requires a careful study of the relevant passages in the Bible. A study of the resurrection passages can make doubters feel right at home because doubt plays a large role in these accounts.

The contradictions among the various gospel accounts can provide other welcome information: Christians have never had just one view of what happened after Jesus died. Many important and easily overlooked factors point to a gradual evolution in the resurrection tradition. St. Paul, whose letters preceded the gospels by at least a generation, does not mention an empty tomb or a visit of angels. The four gospels disagree on important elements as they relate stories about what happened after Jesus died. Matthew places the appearance of Jesus to his disciples in Galilee and Luke in Jerusalem; John has Jesus appear in both places and Mark in neither. These differences suggest that neither Paul nor the gospel writers were producing accounts of an historical event but were offering reflections that demonstrate the impact that Jesus had on their lives. As time passed, these reflections became more elaborate, taking on mythological forms and language. Doubters can find hope through the discovery that no one can take all the details provided by Paul and the gospels and weave them together to form a consistent chronology of events following the death of Jesus.[5] They are not dealing with history but with memory or even myth. As attractive as this kind of Bible study may be to doubters, it can be disturbing to convinced Christians unless they are sufficiently secure in their faith to say, "The details do not matter; what matters is that the lives of the disciples were transformed by the risen Lord, and my life has been transformed, too."

The convinced Christians also can open up the resurrection to the doubtful by suggesting that if they cannot always take the language of the Bible in the most immediate sense of the words, they might look for meaning in metaphors. Resurrection itself can be considered as a metaphor. Two common Greek words in the Bible, which are both translated "rise up," also appear in English as "get up": *anistemi* and *egeiro*. The first means to stand up from a seated or reclining or cowering position. It appears four times in the last chapter of Luke's gospel, twice concerning what happened to Jesus and twice in describing the behavior of disciples. "Peter *got up* and ran to the tomb," and the two disciples from Emmaus, after Jesus appeared to them, "*got up* and returned to Jerusalem." The second word suggests getting yourself (or people, or things) together. It is akin to *agora*, the gathering or marketplace in a Greek town. In the garden of Gethsemane, when Jesus sees Judas and the soldiers coming, he says to his sleeping disciples, "*Get up*, let us be going."[6] We could translate Jesus's command more literally using a contemporary expression, "Get yourselves together; let's get going." Both *anistemi* and *egeiro* are vivid expressions when used metaphorically to describe what happens to people when they encounter Jesus. They discover the capacity to get themselves together, to get up and get going.

In the Bible, resurrection is most often a communal experience. St. Paul frequently used an interesting metaphor in describing the community, an expression that provides a significant link to the resurrection: "Now you are the body of Christ and individually members of it" (1 Cor. 12:27; see also Romans 12:5). Saying that Christ was raised might be taken metaphorically to mean that the disciples got to their feet, that after the death of Jesus they were able to get themselves together and to carry on the work that Jesus had begun.

Doubters can handle metaphors. They hear them everyday and are not troubled by them, nor are they tempted to take them literally. For example, the newspapers reported that the House Ways and Means Committee chairman Dan Rostenkowski said to President Clinton, "Bill, I'm going to be your quarterback and you're my 600-pound gorilla of a fullback moving through these bills." On reading those words, no contemporary American would suppose that the chairman and the president were taking time off to play football any more than they would suppose that president had become a gorilla.

The Problem of Reductionism

Most people can handle metaphors in most contexts, but when it comes to matters of theology many Christians want the words to mean exactly what they seem to say. For people who believe that the raising of Jesus is an historical fact, calling resurrection a metaphor is trivializing the faith. If the resurrection is "just a metaphor," there is no point to being a Christian. They are unmoved by those who say that a metaphor provides the most valid identification of a truth too profound to be expressed by ordinary language used in an ordinary way. Above all they fear "reductionism," simplifying Christian doctrine to the point of minimizing or distorting it. From their point of view, the church does no one a favor by reducing Christian concepts to simpler, more acceptable forms. They are unhappy that so many of their fellow worshipers at present have not grasped the basic gospel message.

A clergyman in the Episcopal Church wrote recently that his denomination received the "worst" marks in a survey that sought to ascertain if, among other things, churchgoers believe they are going to heaven because of God's grace in Jesus's sacrifice on the cross. Only twenty-four percent replied in the affirmative. He suggests that the remaining seventy-six percent need to be evangelized so that they can be prepared to proclaim "the rather specific content of the gospel."[7] But if the saving possibilities proclaimed by the church center on the individual faithful going to heaven when they die, then resurrection becomes an intensely personal concern.

Those who recognize the risks of reductionism can point out that some congregations began to deemphasize the crucifixion at the same time that they began calling the resurrection a metaphor or even a myth. All talk of death and pain, sin and repentance, began to sound ugly and out of place. Liberal preachers recast much of traditional church doctrine in psychological terms, while adult Christian education retreats became almost indistinguishable from any other intensive group encounters. Church members received training in sensitivity and human relations but learned nothing about the Christian tradition. They put aside traditional moral principles and ethical standards in favor of one supreme concern: comfort. "I'm not comfortable with that decision" became the ultimate argument. In congregations that played down the death and resurrection of Jesus, few people were willing to point out that, according to the New Testament, following Jesus inevitably leads to discomfort and even death.

Other congregations reduced the gospel to a call for social action. What people believed and how people behaved did not matter as long as they were willing to serve oppressed minority groups. Churches with a strong emphasis on social action for the most part became social service agencies, using much of their available time and energy in obtaining government grants and in raising money from private sources to carry on their good works among the poor. Most of them have shown little inclination for drawing the people they serve into the life of the worshiping congregation. They have been no more effective in transmitting the Christian tradition than the churches that concentrated on interpersonal relationships.

Not all churches with a reductionist philosophy have suffered a decline in membership. Some have not only kept their members but have grown by becoming community service centers for the suburban middle class and by saying nothing that might cause controversy or offense. They demand no commitment, they provide no discipline, and they offer no challenge. Gary Trudeau gave us a perfect snapshot of these liberal churches in an exchange between Mike Doonesbury and his former college chaplain, who has recently become the pastor of a church. After listening to the pastor describe the programs the church has to deliver for its members—counseling, social events, recovery programs, tutoring, fitness center—Doonesbury asks where God fits into all this. In typical Trudeau fashion, the punch line comes in the penultimate frame: "God? Well, God's still the draw for sure. He's got the big name." The last line can also draw a smile of recognition. When Doonesbury asks if they ever evoke God's name anymore, the response is: "Um...Frankly, Mike, God comes with a lot of baggage. The whole male, Euro-centric, guilt thing."[8]

Any congregation that attempts to include doubters in its program of evangelism runs the risk of falling into the reductionist trap, but convinced Christians can find ways to carry on the task of intelligent evangelism while staying clear of the pitfalls. Some years ago, I was working on a series of community life conferences with a colleague who has much the same approach as I and with another clergyman who considered himself to be much more conservative. After an evening session at one of the weekend conferences, he exploded, "You guys had me fooled! I thought you were liberals. You're not liberal at all. You're more conservative than I am. You're the John Birch Society of the church. You take the Bible seriously. You even take worship and tradition seriously." His words—half admiring, half accusing—have stayed with me. Anyone who attempts to bring into the church people who have problems with organized religion must be diligent in the study of the Bible, responsible in the conduct of public worship, and conscientious in the maintenance of tradition in order to make an honest presentation of both the promises and demands of the gospel.

If a congregation decides to run the risk of reductionism, along with the other risks attached to a program of evangelism among secular people, the members still must deal with the upsets that will occur as they adapt their style, their organization, and their ways of thinking to make outsiders feel welcome. In making such adaptations, they may take courage from the knowledge that Christians who have gone before them went through similar upsets for the sake of evangelism.

Part Two

Chapter 5

Adjusting the Message for the Sake of the Mission

L et us assume that a certain congregation has weighed the costs and promises of a commitment to evangelism and has decided to proceed. Its leaders are ready to develop a strategy designed to welcome outsiders and let these newcomers know what this congregation has found of value in belonging to a Christian community. Before going on, however, they might do well to pause and learn what they can from the history of Christian missions.

The best place to start is with St. Paul. Although the author of Acts never calls St. Paul an evangelist, the book presents his work as the primary example of what evangelism is supposed to be, a constant adaptation of the gospel to fit changing circumstances. When St. Paul arrived in Athens, he started arguing with Jews and other devout persons in the synagogue and with the philosophers in the marketplace. According to the Acts of the Apostles, Paul had better luck in the marketplace than in the synagogue—at least some of the people there wanted to hear more from him. Paul took advantage of this opportunity, and began his presentation by saying, "Athenians, I see how extremely religious you are in every way." In this case, he began his work in a new city by debating with the guardians of his own tradition and their devout followers. Keeping in contact with the more conservative factions of a religious movement, even if contact produces unresolved arguments, may be an important principle put forward in the story. Another principle may be to begin with whatever you can affirm in the position taken by the outsiders you are trying to reach. Acknowledging that they are genuinely religious people could be just the opening you need.

Throughout the ages Christians have adjusted both the form and the content of their message for the sake of evangelism. Because some of the believers were eager to get the word to new groups of people while others were concerned about preserving the integrity of the faith, most adjustments have provoked controversy within the established Christian communities. If we can learn anything at all from our history, it is that anyone promoting evangelism should be prepared for resistance and conflict. From our history we also might pick up some clues that will suggest how we might best take advantage of the opportunities for evangelism in our times and how we might most constructively deal with the controversy we provoke within the church.

Adapting Christianity to Different Cultures

According to a tradition reflected in the Acts of the Apostles, the first attempt of the Jesus followers to adapt their message to a new culture occurred when they welcomed Hellenistic Jews into their community. Jesus and all his followers were Palestinian Jews who spoke a dialect called Aramaic. Those who could write used the Hebrew alphabet, but most of them could not speak the Hebrew language; they only heard it in the synagogue when someone read from the ancient scriptures. Although their language had evolved over the generations, as spoken languages always do, the culture of the Palestinian peasants had remained constant for centuries, in spite of wars and occupation by foreign troops. They lived in small farming or fishing villages and carried on with their lives in much the same fashion as their ancestors.

Not all Jews had remained attached to their native villages, however. Nations that had conquered their little country had carried some of them into exile, and others had left voluntarily in search of better economic opportunities. In time, Jews had become dispersed throughout the Mediterranean basin and even beyond. Being occupied in commerce, many of them had adopted the *lingua Franca* of the business world—common Greek. Scholars among them eventually translated the Hebrew scriptures into Greek, and by the time of Jesus many of the Jews outside of Palestine knew the Bible only in this Greek version. Although they observed the Jewish laws of circumcision, dress, and diet, they were thoroughly hellenized in most other respects. They had adopted not only the Greek language, but most aspects of Greek culture as well. They acted like Greeks; they thought like Greeks. In contrast to the Jews who had remained in Palestine, those who had scattered had settled mostly in cities. They were urban people, different from the peasant farmers and fisherfolk who had listened to Jesus and had decided to follow him.

The fact that Acts mentions a conflict between Palestinian and Hellenistic Jews in the Jesus movement suggests a problem that may have been a widespread clash between two cultures in the church. The first mention of the controversy appears in the sixth chapter:

> Now during those days, when the disciples were increasing in number, the Hellenists complained against the Hebrews because their widows were being neglected in the daily distribution of food. (Acts 6:1)

According to this account, the twelve men who governed the church solved the problem by appointing seven men chosen by the Greek-speaking members of the community to take care of the food distribution so the twelve could devote themselves "to prayer and to serving the word." This neat division of labor between those who would manage the food and those who would serve the word may have existed solely in the imagination of the author of Acts, for the only activities reported of the seven who had been appointed to "wait on tables" were preaching and teaching. Stephen immediately began preaching about Jesus in a synagogue attended by other Hellenistic Jews, and Philip was soon off preaching in Samaria.

Apparently at the time Acts was written, the Christian community still retained a clear memory that the original followers of Jesus had encountered problems in an attempt to include Hellenistic Jews. Their cultures were so different that the two groups did not mix easily. The solution was to create parallel organizational structures so that each could have its own leaders and so that each could carry on the business of evangelism primarily among its own kind of people. Some churches in the suburbs of Washington, D.C., have had to make similar accommodations in their parish organizations to incorporate those who have recently arrived from Africa. American-born church members were used to having all church meetings on weeknights, while the Africans expected to spend all day Sunday at church, taking care of any necessary church business on that one day. Even though total integration of the two cultures remains the ideal, new African members are not likely to show up for weeknight meetings and long-time parishioners are not going to spend the whole of Sunday at church.

In a similar fashion, if a conservative church successfully recruits a number of questioning types, they may find that the newer group does not mix very well with the ones who have been around for fifteen or twenty years. For this reason, some congregations have established two major services on Sunday morning, one that emphasizes predictability and reassurance and one that provokes thought and encourages questions. Following the same pattern, congregations have provided two kinds of educational experiences for adults, those that offer information and those that invite reflection and analysis. Christians often worry if a congregation does not appear to be one, big, happy family, but the principle of parallel structures dramatized in Acts may sometimes produce the best results for the most people.

An even greater controversy arose when the Hellenistic Jews in the church began admitting people who were not even Jewish—not only Greeks and Romans but people from a variety of other ethnic groups. In the letters of St. Paul we have only one side of the argument that erupted between him and the leadership of the church in Jerusalem over his decision that these gentiles who wanted to follow Jesus did not first have to become Jews. Paul and the other Hellenistic Jews who had become Christians knew a great many gentiles who had become skeptical about their own religious traditions and had become curious about Judaism. These gentiles were attracted to the high moral principles and the dynamic monotheism they discovered by attending synagogues, but they did not want to become Jews. Most of them did not want to adopt the distinctive dress and diet of the Jews, and the men did not want to be circumcised, a particularly embarrassing and painful operation for an adult.

Paul and his friends decided to welcome them into the church just as they were, a decision that apparently caused no end of upset for the Jesus followers in Jerusalem. They sent emissaries around to the congregations that had admitted gentiles, insisting that the men must all be circumcised. Paul vigorously defended the evangelistic strategy that he and his associates had adopted, insisting in his letter to the Galatians that he "had been entrusted with the gospel for the uncircumcised, just as Peter had been entrusted with the gospel for the circumcised." Eventually his views prevailed. He was so successful that by the fourth century the Jewish followers of Jesus in Palestine had become isolated from the rest of the church and their views branded as heresy.[1]

By opening their doors first to Hellenistic Jews, who then admitted gentiles, the original followers of Jesus made possible the rapid expansion of Christianity, but in the process they lost control over the movement. A congregation that attempts to include people of another culture runs the same risk; the new people may take over. In one congregation people still talk about a meeting over thirty years ago at which the new, younger, and better educated group challenged the official slate for parish offices with a slate of their own. When they discovered that they had won, a few of the victors were horrified to realize that in the process of taking over they had ousted their best friend among the older crowd, but they were not half so upset as the long-time members, many of whom felt betrayed and angry. Fortunately for the health of the congregation, the new people's one friend in the establishment, whom they had just defeated, stood up at the end of the meeting and said simply, "I'll be here on Sunday."

The original group also risks the loss of their cultural identity in the process of adapting themselves to the culture of the people they are trying to reach. In the congregation just mentioned, once the newer group was in charge, the church rapidly changed its character. From a group with largely unexamined beliefs and simple tastes, the congregation had become a gathering of people who took pride in their intellectual achievements and skeptical attitudes. In the process, some of the life-long members left because they no longer felt at home in their church. Others, with varying degrees of success, tried to talk and behave like the newcomers.

St. Paul apparently accepted the risks of either losing control or losing his cultural identity. Whether dealing with his fellow Jews or with gentiles, Paul's method of evangelism remained the same. He adapted himself to the style and culture of others rather than encouraging them to be like him.

> To the Jews I became as a Jew, in order to win Jews. To those under the law I became as one under the law (though I myself am not under the law) so that I might win those under the law. To those outside the law I became as one outside the law (though I am not free from God's law but am under Christ's law) so that I might win those outside the law. To the weak I became weak, so that I might win the weak. I have become all things to all people, that I might by all means save some. I do it all for the sake of the gospel, so that I may share in its blessings. (1 Cor. 9:20-23)

How far should Christians go in adapting themselves to other cultures for the sake of the gospel? That is the question all evangelists must ask themselves. As we know, the need to adapt to a prevailing culture did not end with St. Paul.

Just consider how the first Christian missionaries in Great Britain and northern Europe approached the annual indigenous festivals celebrated by the people they encountered. Until Christianity moved beyond the eastern shores of the Mediterranean Sea, Christians observed the Jewish holy days and seasons based on the agricultural cycle of the region, giving each festival their own special twist. At the time of the barley harvest, when the Jews celebrated Passover, the Jewish followers of Jesus remembered his death and the new life his death made possible. At the time of the wheat harvest, when the Jews celebrated God's gift of the Torah to Moses and the people of Israel, the Jewish followers of Jesus remembered the founding of their new community and the gift of God's spirit among them, calling the day by the name Hellenistic Jews had long used, Pentecost.

When Christians moved farther north, they discovered that the harvests occurred in the fall but that the people in those lands also had festivals at the equinox and in May. In adapting the customs of the church to the existing celebration at the time of the vernal equinox, the missionaries to the Germanic tribes did not even bother to change the name of the festival. They continued to call the day "Easter," the name of the goddess of fertility. Although they did manage to change the name of the later spring celebration from Beltane to

Pentecost, missionaries allowed their new followers to carry on much as they always had.

The missionaries also discovered that in the north the greater contrast between the brief hours of daylight in the winter and the long days of summer had created a need for some kind of celebration around the time of the winter solstice. As soon as people could see that darkness had not overpowered the sun, they expressed their joy with eating and drinking and singing, and with fires and evergreens to remind themselves that the light would return in force and that the earth would be green once more. Not having any idea when Jesus was born, the Christian missionaries kept the festival; they just changed the name to Christmas. These celebrations, especially Christmas and Easter, are so much a part of our culture that we can easily overlook the radical nature of their adoption by Christian missionaries for the sake of evangelism.

Although the spiritual descendants of John Calvin and the Puritans have stopped denouncing as pagan the customs surrounding Christmas and Easter, some churches still condemn the customs attached to October 31, the eve of All Saints' Day, otherwise known as All Hallows' Eve or Halloween. For Celtic people, the new year began on November 1. Christians were so successful in adapting this existing festival to their purposes that All Saints' Day and the old Celtic custom of the evil spirits walking the earth the night before spread throughout Christendom. As we listen to some contemporary Christian preachers denouncing Halloween, we can get some idea of the controversy that must have been stirred up each time a group of Christians tried to adapt their message to the existing festivals of a different culture.[2]

In the light of the adaptations to indigenous festivals made by evangelists, the suggestion that Christians today fit their message to the culture of intellectual inquiry may not seem so radical. If Christians in the past could affirm and encourage the expressions of conviction that they found in the existing celebrations of different cultures, their counterparts today need not shrink from affirming and encouraging a skeptical attitude toward the supernatural. By joining in the festivals, the missionaries in the past showed their respect for the people to whom they were bringing their message. In the same fashion, modern evangelists can show their respect for secular culture by joining the doubters in their questioning of religious doctrines.

What little evidence we have suggests that these early adaptations of Christianity to new cultures were part of a carefully worked out strategy of evangelism. The Venerable Bede, writing in the eighth century, quoted at some length the directions Pope Gregory the Great had sent from Rome one hundred thirty or forty years earlier to Augustine, his missionary in Britain. Concerning the English, Gregory sent word that "the idol temples of that race should by no means be destroyed, but only the idols in them. Take holy water and sprinkle it in these shrines, build altars and place relics in them." He reasoned that these were perfectly good buildings, which were "familiar" places for the people to assemble. He dealt with animal sacrifice in a similarly conciliatory manner. Because the people were used to offering animal sacrifices, "some solemnity ought to be given them in exchange" for what they had given up. He suggested that the missionaries organize great feasts on the Christian festivals. "It is doubtless impossible to cut out everything at once from their stubborn minds: just as the man who is attempting to climb to the highest places, rises by steps and degrees and not by leaps."[3] Respecting the culture and religious practices of a people in missionary territory was a sensible strategy, and it worked. Because of Gregory's strategy, the church in England is a blend of the old Anglo-Saxon observances and the newer Christian practices.

Sometimes Christians have changed their approach not so much to adapt themselves to a different culture but to supply a missing element. Early in the nineteenth century, when Christianity crossed over the Appalachian mountains and moved west with the pioneers, women formed alliances with their pastors to create a social order that would offer them and their children some economic protection. On the frontier of European civilization in North America, if men got their hands on any money, they were accustomed to drinking it up or gambling it away. Most of the men did not appear to be much interested in religion, so to get established in the new communities, pastors were willing to support the women by denouncing drinking and gambling. For many practicing Christians, the opposition of the church to the use of alcoholic beverages came as something of a shock, since the central sacrament of the church required the use of wine—or at least it did until 1869, when Dr. Thomas Bramwell Welch, a communion steward in the Vineland, New Jersey, Methodist church, developed a process of pasteurizing grape juice to keep it from fermenting. Early Baptist clergy sometimes received their compensation in barrels of whiskey, and the definition of a "hard-shell Baptist" was one who would not leave home without a bottle of whiskey in his saddle bags. Card playing and horse racing were among the few amusements available, and most men did not find these diversions very amusing unless they had money riding on the outcome. But for the sake of the mission, the Christian clergy joined the women in a drive to protect family interests by opposing both drinking and gambling.[4]

Times and needs change. Many unsuccessful churches in urban areas carry on their crusade against drinking and gambling as if they were still operating in frontier villages. In the late 1960s, the executives of one denomination sent an experienced and dynamic clergyman to Washington, D.C., to see if he could help ten dwindling congregations find new life. After looking over the situation in the residential areas of Capitol Hill, he announced that in twenty-five years the only surviving churches would be Episcopal—a prophecy based on the lifestyles of the people moving into recently renovated townhouses in the neighborhood. They may not have been interested in gambling, but most of them wanted a drink after work and found the church's ban on drinking at social functions deeply hypocritical. Even the recovering alcoholics, he predicted, would not want to join a church that made drinking a sin instead of a problem. His prophecy has not proved to be entirely accurate, but while several churches have closed and others are struggling for survival, the Episcopal churches have prospered.

Adapting Christianity to Popular Ways of Thinking

Besides adjusting their ways of doing things for the sake of evangelism, Christians over the ages have also engaged in the more demanding task of changing their ways of thinking. To get their message across, evangelists have done their best to understand how their target audiences think and have tried to express their message in forms that will be familiar to them. In trying to learn from their predecessors, today's Christians will always have to ask themselves if the changes preserved or distorted the message proclaimed by Jesus. Any attempt to speak directly to the needs and desires of the listener risks the possibility that the evangelist may be holding out a false savior.

The process of putting the message in forms that people could grasp began with Jesus and continued after his death. Jesus told parables with characters and events that would have been familiar to the Palestinian peasants to whom he spoke. The author of the letter to the Hebrews combined the rich imagery of temple worship with Platonic philosophy, perhaps in an attempt to reach a sophisticated Jewish audience. St. Paul used metaphors derived from sporting events, such as boxing and foot races, to make himself clear to his Greek and Roman correspondents. Each of the four gospels was written for a particular group of people and had a slightly different message. Matthew appears to have been written for people with a familiarity with the Hebrew scriptures, while Luke seems to be somewhat slanted toward a more thoroughly gentile audience. Mark may have been written for people who already knew something about the teachings of Jesus but needed his story in a concise form, perhaps for educational or liturgical purposes. John seems to have been aimed at the already committed Christians whose faith was wavering in the turbulent times after the destruction of the temple, when the Jesus followers were no longer welcome in the synagogues.

At times, advocates for Christianity have simultaneously adapted themselves to contradictory ways of thinking that they discovered within a culture. In the seventh century, for example, the Celtic monks from Iona found that the Anglo-Saxon men thought about religion primarily in terms of war and the women in terms of peace and stability. They were able to establish a permanent base of operations among the English who had settled north of the Humber River because they convinced Oswald, who became king of Northumbria, that the God they worshiped was powerful in battle, scattering his enemies like chaff before the wind. The night before a major battle Oswald had a vision of St. Columba, who offered him technical advice: attack in the dark. Oswald won a great victory and, according to the Venerable Bede, he invited the elders from Iona to send monks who could help him. He "was anxious that the whole race under his rule should be filled with the grace of the Christian faith of which he had so wonderful an experience in overcoming the barbarians."

The Christian god soon replaced the old Anglo-Saxon gods of war, Thor and Woden, but the new god of war would not have appealed to Anglo-Saxon women. The monks of Iona preached the god of love, whose son was the prince of peace. The success of Christian evangelism among the English was largely the result of the alliance between the monks and the women of noble birth. The monks encouraged these talented women to pursue their interests in scholarship and management, and soon women established their own monastic institutions that became centers of learning and of the arts, such as the monastery of Hilda at Whitby. Her position in the church and society, and that of women like her, was made possible by the monks who were willing to accommodate their message to meet the ways that women needed to exercise leadership, ways that were different from those of the men, who had little on their minds but warfare.

Other people in more peaceful times and places have tried to make sense out of things through philosophy. Where evangelism has been successful, the advocates for Christianity have expressed their message in the categories of whatever philosophy was most popular among the people with whom they were working. For centuries, in Europe the most widely accepted approach to philosophy was that set out by Plato, but by the thirteenth century all people did not find the Platonic idealisms a congenial way of expressing themselves. Many educated people had become attracted to Aristotle's emphasis on experience and common sense as the way to knowledge. Although scholars in the church had been studying Aristotle for some years, it took the efforts of a young rebel, whose name was Thomas Aquinas, to recast the Christian message in Aristotelian categories. Because the writings of Thomas Aquinas have provided the basis for Roman Catholic theology since the sixteenth century, it is easy to forget the controversy these works provoked when they were first circulated: bishops and archbishops condemned several propositions that they found in the teachings of Thomas, and for a time the Franciscan Order actually forbade its members to study any of Thomas's work. The conflict that Thomas Aquinas provoked among the authorities in the church should remind anyone of the risks to be run in an attempt to recast Christian theology in new philosophical categories.

Fortunately for the cause of evangelism, many theologians in modern times have been willing to take the risk. Before World War I, scholars such as Adolf von Harnack presented Jesus as an historical figure who could appeal to the liberal, optimistic ways of thinking that dominated the western world. After people's confidence in an ever-improving world collapsed in the rubble of the war, other interpreters of Christianity appeared on the scene who used other categories. One of them was Paul Tillich. He employed the insights of depth psychology in making the case for Christianity, examining the threat of "non-being" as the motivation behind the religious quest. After World War II, some Christian writers began using Marxist categories in developing a theology of liberation, while others presented their message in terms of existentialism or logical positivism.

Adapting Christianity to the Philosophy of Acquisition

In adapting Christianity to popular ways of thinking, the members of any congregation will face a complex task because at any given moment they will be dealing with people who represent a wide range of strong yet unarticulated "philosophies." Acquisition is one of the most powerful philosophies at work in our culture; people find meaning in their attempts to acquire wealth, status, or power. If they think at all about what they are doing, they will take for granted that what matters in this life is money, social position, or control over other people. Conventional evangelists who understand this kind of thinking assume they have two options: either they can offer Christianity as the means to more effective ways of acquiring what the heart desires, or they can try to expose the ultimate emptiness of a life based on acquisition.

Evangelists who have given evangelism a bad reputation sometimes have been effective in making use of the former. Their disciples testify that they have succeeded in business or politics because of their faith, such as the hairdresser who told me that he had struggled for years just to keep his business afloat. Then one day he responded to a preacher and accepted Jesus Christ as his personal Lord and Savior. From that moment on he began to prosper. He told me that he now owned a chain of beauty shops, all of which were doing well. Because he owed his prosperity to God, each week he gave ten percent of his profits to the church. Conventional evangelists who take the other approach can point to the opposite kind of success; their followers can testify to the shallowness of their goals and the vacuous nature of their lives until they found religion.

The pursuit of pleasure is closely related to acquisition as a way of finding meaning. For some people wealth has value only because it makes possible the purchase of what gives pleasure. Others find that the effort and responsibilities that go with wealth rob them of their pleasure. In either case what matters is good feelings—"If it feels good, do it," as people used to say. Although one seldom hears that philosophy of life stated so baldly nowadays, many people still assume that it is the only guiding principle for life that makes sense. For others the philosophy only makes sense if stated in the negative: "If it feels bad, avoid it." I have seen the work of governing boards come to a standstill when one member complains, "I'm not comfortable with that decision." Whole industries have developed to help people overcome stress, strain, and burnout. Conventional evangelists can join the movement and offer religion as the way to really good feelings, especially feelings about yourself. They can show how prayer can relieve the tension in your life. Or they can take the opposite approach and help people find meaning in their suffering and distress. Although intelligent evangelists must avoid the extremes of both approaches, they should realize that the pursuit of pleasure and the avoidance of discomfort as some people's only philosophy of life.

Before taking a serious look at Christianity, some people have already discovered the hollowness of any self-centered philosophy of life and have looked for meaning in a third possibility: the service of humankind. Although at first glance doing things for people seems different from self-centered acquisition, closer scrutiny will disclose a basic similarity in the two philosophies. Both provide ways of investing life with meaning, and the value in each instance appears to be self-evident to the doer. People who consider themselves to be altruists would be horrified to find themselves in the same category with those they think are leading lives driven by greed, but the evangelist must understand that a philosophy of life based on activism produces similar results. A probation officer discouraged with her attempts at helping convicted felons become contributing members of society may be in a state similar to that of the bonds trader who no longer finds satisfaction in making a multimillion dollar deal. In trying to make welcome those who try to live for others, evangelists have the same options as they do in working with the acquisitive types. Any sensitive evangelist would offer the church as a place of encouragement and support for those who serve; the next step would be to help people discover the ultimate hopelessness of trying to create meaning through activity, even service to others.

Often people turn to family or community as a source of meaning, believing that the meaning of life will be found in human relationships. Once evangelists understand this way of thinking, they can frame their invitation in a way that suggests that the church can help a couple cope with both their children and their aging parents, as well as with each other. The church can help a single person develop skills in making and keeping friendships in order to avoid isolation and loneliness. Evangelists can also help people realize that they will never straighten out all their relationships and that neither family nor community can ultimately make their lives worthwhile.

The work of effective evangelism under such conditions involves a three-step process that begins with helping prospective members put into words the philosophy they have used in trying to make sense out of their lives. The second step involves showing them how they can understand Christianity in terms of their personal philosophy and how the church can support them in what they are already doing. In the third step, the church encourages people to question the assumptions and conclusions they arrived at in step two. By emphasizing the importance of the questions, the church can help people understand that any philosophy, any way of thinking, can be a false savior, a substitute for God.

Any congregation that attempts to present the gospel in these terms will, of course, be subject to the negative criticism of Christians who think that the only way to get across the message is to tell people what they must believe in order to be saved. They will be accused of selling out to the culture, of being merely "trendy." Adjusting the message for the sake of the mission has always provoked an outcry of protest and always will.

Adapting Church Organization to Changing Conditions

In getting the message across, the way a church organizes itself may be as important as the way it expresses itself. Even in the first century following the death of Jesus, the church seems to have been experimenting with structures that were different from other organizations. People who study the surviving letters of St. Paul are often surprised to learn that the early church seems to have had no hierarchy and that authority was shared equally among men and women.[5] A century later, when the letters to Timothy and Titus were written, the organization was changing. The church had developed the position of *episcopos*, literally "overseer," but now translated "bishop." The office of bishop was restricted to men, and women were limited to supportive or even subservient roles. The change in structure may well have been the result of a desire for more effective evangelism. The early church's democratic structure, with its emphasis on equality among all the followers of Jesus, may well have scandalized middle-class Roman citizens who believed that a woman should always be subject to the authority of a man, either her father or her husband. They also would tend to distrust any organization that did not have most of the features with which they were familiar in the Roman military and civil branches of government.

By adopting a Roman organizational system while it was still an underground movement in the second and third centuries, the church positioned itself for rapid expansion in the fourth century when the emperor Constantine removed the legal restrictions on Christianity. In the succeeding decades, as effective Roman control began to disintegrate in the face of barbarian incursions, in many places the bishops took on responsibilities for governing the state as well as the church. Each bishop had a "see," a geographical center for his activities, in a city that had been the site of the ancient Roman administration of the province. Bishops and other clergy eventually adopted the dress originally worn by officials of the empire, complete with insignia and regalia, reminding their people that in the church power flowed from the top—the bishop of Rome—down through the other bishops and priests to the ordinary Christian.

Not all Christians were pleased by the church taking on the trappings of power, especially when men corrupted the organization by seeking positions in the hierarchy as a means of gaining wealth and status. To protest the corruption, some Christians fled the cities to find places of refuge in deserted areas at the remote edges of the empire, where they could devote themselves to a simple life of contemplative prayer. In spite of the corruption and the protests, the centralized organization proved to be effective in spreading Christianity throughout the remains of the empire and beyond.

Educated, urban people tend to distrust people in power, especially those whose authority goes unquestioned. For evangelism to have a chance with those who are skeptical about organized religion, the congregation must adapt whatever structure it may have inherited to meet their suspicions. Concentrating authority in the hands of an attractive cleric can be an effective tool of evangelism among insecure people who long for someone to tell them what to think, what to believe, and what to do. In attempting to attract questioning people, however, the evangelizing church must adapt to a style of intense participatory democracy: open elections, open discussion of issues, open decision-making.

For congregations with a long history of avoiding conflict, adapting themselves to a more open style of organization can both unleash energy and cause discomfort. People who run for office and win can experience genuine affirmation, but those who lose can feel rejected. When differences of opinion come out into the open, people may enjoy the stimulation of healthy arguments, or they may become anxious about the possibility of separation and alienation. If a vote in a board meeting is recorded, those on both sides of the issue may have to answer for the positions they took. The prospect of dealing with the people who revel in their new-found authority and with those upset by an open system may be difficult for the clergy, but they may also appreciate the strength they derive from collegiality. The congregation and clergy together will have to weigh the positive and the negative possibilities before deciding how to adapt their current organization to meet the challenge of evangelism.

Down through the ages, each time a Christian community has decided to spread the gospel, church members have faced similar decisions. A congregation that becomes serious about evangelism will always experience the challenge of figuring out how to adapt itself to a different culture, different ways of thinking, and different expectations about organization and authority. If the congregation makes adjustments, then it will benefit from the stimulation that the changes themselves will inevitably generate. As difficult as the adaptations may be, the most daunting challenges will probably release the most energy and produce the most new life. The members of the congregation may face the most daunting challenge of all when they try to explain what the church has to offer people who come with doubts and questions, and a need to analyze all that they hear. This is the test that holds the greatest potential for the congregation's discovery of new meaning in the gospel.

Chapter 6

Offering a Gospel of
Freedom and Responsibility

D uring the early sixties, when the churches were just beginning to question their successful expansion in the pre-
vious decade, I heard a story about a researcher who took
a tape recorder with her to the homes of active church members and
asked them, "What is the message your church has to offer?" When
she played back the results of her survey to the church leadership,
more often than not all they heard following the question was the
quiet hiss of the tape. Along with everyone else who heard that story,
I began to wonder how the church could sustain itself if even its own
members could not describe what welcome news their congregation
might have for outsiders.

Before a congregation can adapt its message to new circumstances, the membership must have some idea of what they mean by
"gospel." To make their gospel available to people with serious questions, a congregation must be able to describe "the good message"
in a way that allows people to make a positive response but that does
not put them under pressure to accept particular religious beliefs.

The gospel message cannot be delivered, however, without a clear
statement of what will be demanded of those who accept it. People
will accept the gospel only if they hear an outrageous promise, but
they will never experience the promise unless they can accept the
outrageous demand that the gospel includes. As a matter of strategy,
the outrageous promise must always precede the outrageous demand, but in reality the two are inseparable. In preparing for a program of evangelism, a congregation will have to clarify what they

have to offer and what they will demand of those who respond favorably.

Although gospel, *euangelion*, literally meant good message or good news, in Jesus's time rulers sometimes used the word to identify proclamations of freedom, such as a general amnesty for the vanquished after a conquest was complete.[1] Such a proclamation carried an explicit or implied set of responsibilities for those who accepted the freedoms offered. If the church publishes a similar proclamation of freedom in the name of its Lord, the members must be prepared to answer the questions "Freedom from what?" and "Freedom for what?" The gospel announced by Jesus of Nazareth does not seem to have been primarily about political freedom or being set free from jail, but rather about a freedom realized from within, a liberation from mental and emotional prisons. An unbeliever can feel just as trapped as any believer; both may long for freedom without knowing what they are seeking.

Although human beings can imprison their spirits in a great variety of ways, three strike me as particularly insidious: the burdens of guilt and shame, the oppression of fate, and the chaos of emptiness. In every case people may feel like the helpless victims of circumstances, but they may also come to discover the extent to which their choices in the past led to their present condition. With the realization of personal responsibility comes the freedom to choose different responses to circumstances in the future.

The Burdens of Shame and Guilt

For most of us shame and guilt are synonymous, but psychotherapists make a useful distinction between the two. Guilt is the existential condition of being in the wrong and the bad feelings that arise from having done something wrong or having failed to do what is right, while shame is feeling bad about who you are. The two sets of feelings get mixed up because they often occur simultaneously. For example, a high school teacher who was talking to his students about infectious diseases told them that malaria was caused by a virus. The next day one of his students announced to the class that her mother, a physician, said that malaria was not caused by a virus but a parasite. When the dictionary on his desk proved that his student was correct, the teacher experienced a moment of both guilt and shame. He was guilty of a failure to do his homework, to check his facts before making a presentation. He also felt ashamed of himself for not being the kind of teacher he meant to be. He was sure that he had lost stature in the eyes of the class, as he had in his own estimation.

People often have trouble discussing guilt because they confuse guilty feelings with the actual state of being guilty. One person can feel guilty without having done anything wrong, while another can misbehave and not feel guilty at all. The teacher's guilt was genuine; he had misled the class because he had not prepared adequately. His feelings of guilt pointed to the reality of his failure to live up to the standards of his profession that he had accepted for himself. He did not just feel guilty; he was guilty. His guilt was not a psychological but an existential condition.

The teacher's sense of shame erupted alongside of the guilt largely because of his early training. More than once he had turned on the television before completing all his math problems, and his mother had said, "You know the rule. No TV until your homework is finished. You should be ashamed of yourself." Throughout his life, whenever he tried to enjoy himself before completing his work, he felt the shame. Even if parents do not use the language of shame, they do their best to help their children develop a set of internal controls so that they can function acceptably with other people. Whenever the internal controls fail to operate, the parents let the children know that their performance was not acceptable. Shame is the feeling of being unacceptable.

Normally guilt and shame function effectively as early warning devices that help people from getting into the kind of trouble that will cause them to be alienated from particular individuals or from society as a whole. Under most conditions, if friends suggested an evening of drinking Guinness and listening to Irish music at a local pub, the teacher would decline the invitation rather than show up at class the next morning unprepared. When a college classmate, who was going to be in the city for just one night, showed up with a similar invitation, however, the teacher decided to disregard the early warning signals and suffered the consequences the next day, mistakenly calling a parasite a virus. If such minor lapses occur infre-

quently and the teacher does not worry about them, shame and guilt
are not burdens but assets.

Guilt can be a terrible burden and so can shame if the teacher becomes aware of a developing pattern of late-night socializing and inadequate preparation for class. If the situation becomes sufficiently
serious, but the teacher seems unable to break out of the pattern,
the possibility of freedom might come as good news, especially if the
news includes the steps he might take in claiming his liberation. If
the teacher is a typical questioning type, the person from the church
trying to bring him the message would not try to start a conversation
with the appropriate verse from the gospels. The bearer of the message would do well to internalize the message in its original form
and to find new ways of expressing it:

> Now after John was arrested, Jesus came to Galilee, proclaiming the
> good news of God, and saying, "The time is fulfilled, and the kingdom of God has come near; repent, and believe in the good news."
> (Mark 1:14-15)

If Jesus intended the "good news *(euangelion)* of God" to be a proclamation of freedom for people imprisoned by guilt and shame, he
held out hope to those who were willing to accept two responsibilities. The first is to repent, and the second is to believe in the proclamation.

The Greek word translated "repent" is *metanoeo*, which means to
change your mind or to change your attitude. If the teacher feels
trapped in a pattern that continually produces guilt and shame, one
place to begin would be an examination of his attitudes, toward work
and toward socializing. What has happened to the enthusiasm he
once had about teaching? What has caused him to become almost
desperate in his desire to be out with friends each evening? The
teacher can see that he will find no relief from his burdensome feelings without a change in attitude, but few people can produce an attitude change by deciding to do so, no matter how determined they
are to have a different mind-set. They need something more.

According to Mark's gospel, to have a change in attitude people
must "believe in the good news." One important connotation of the
Greek word translated "believe in" can best be expressed as "have
confidence in," and Mark reports that Jesus taught people to have

confidence in the proclamation of freedom. The realm of God is breaking in. People do not have to think of themselves as trapped by the present order of things, which includes the patterns of behavior that have been causing them misery. They can develop confidence in a new reality. They can imagine the new reality to be something like a sovereign for the whole universe declaring that everyone has been set free from shame and guilt.

Those who choose to accept their emancipation soon discover its accompanying responsibilities; they find that they have been set free to straighten out their relationships with other people. This straightening out process the Bible sometimes calls "reconciliation," a word that suggests that further change might be in order:

> So when you are offering your gift at the altar, if you remember that your brother or sister has something against you, leave your gift there before the altar and go; first be reconciled to your brother or sister, and then come and offer your gift. (Matthew 5:23-24)

These words that Matthew attributes to Jesus take for granted that the readers will know what a willingness to "be reconciled" means. According to the Torah, the first step is to make restitution, if that is possible. If the offense is wrongfully holding a deposit, or taking something by fraud or theft, the person seeking reconciliation is to return the principal amount plus one fifth (Leviticus 6:1-7). Some people who read the passage today assume that reconciliation also included asking for forgiveness from the person with something against you, but nothing in the Bible would support that assumption. None of the gospels suggests that Jesus ever urged people to ask those whom they offended to forgive them. In all the advice that St. Paul so readily offered in his letters that have survived, not once did he urge his readers to ask other people for forgiveness. In the Hebrew scriptures, only twice do we find people asking other people to forgive them, and in one case the request was not even genuine. When Abigail learned that David was going to destroy everything she held dear because her husband Nabal had insulted some of David's men, she tried to put the blame on herself and asked David to forgive her.

In the Bible, the only other plea for a human being to forgive an offense resulted in an absolute but well-reasoned refusal. After the death of the patriarch Jacob, or Israel as he came to be called, his older sons were afraid that their brother Joseph would decide to take his revenge upon them for selling him into slavery when he was a young man. The brothers came to Joseph and begged him to forgive their crime and the wrong they had done in harming him, but Joseph said to them, "Do not be afraid! Am I in the place of God?" Only God can forgive. By asking Joseph to forgive them, his brothers were putting Joseph in the place of God. People who ask another person to forgive an offense are putting the other person in control of their souls' health, in charge of their spiritual well-being. They are turning over to human beings authority that belongs to God, asking them to do what God alone can do, and in the process creating a barrier to reconciliation.

A busy executive who has promised her husband that for once on a Friday night she would be home in time for dinner with him and the children arrives long after dinner is over, the dishes washed, and the children put to bed. If she asks her husband to forgive her, she puts him in an impossible position and creates further problems for herself. Even if he does not fully comprehend the implications of a request to forgive her, he will sense that she has given him the power to make her feel better about her failure to keep an agreement, a power that could corrupt the marriage bond. Yet at their marriage service they had prayed that when they hurt each other they would "seek each other's forgiveness." How is seeking forgiveness different from asking to be forgiven?

Although granting another person the authority to release you from the misery you have created by your offenses or lapses will impede reconciliation, you can seek forgiveness by offering an apology or saying that you are sorry. If you can do so within the original meaning of those terms, you will not be asking another person to make you feel better. An apology, or *apologia,* was originally a strong defense of a position taken and did not carry an admission of fault. Sometimes it helps to explain what you did and why you did it and to let the other person decide if your explanation has cleared up the trouble between you. You also can say you are sorry, if indeed looking back at your behavior makes you sad, or sore at heart. If your sorrow was produced by the other person's upset over what you did or did not do, rather than by a reflection on your actions, then saying you are sorry probably will not help with reconciliation. Nor will saying that you are sorry do much good if you do not feel at all sad about your conduct. Only an honest statement about your feelings toward your past behavior will allow the other person to see your willingness to be reconciled.

Another popular misconception about reconciliation entails a willingness to forgive yourself. If you are looking for wisdom in the Bible to guide your actions, you will look in vain for any suggestion that forgiving yourself is an appropriate way to get out from under the burdens of guilt and shame. The Bible does not mention the subject directly, but I think it is safe to say that any author or editor who contributed to either the Hebrew or Christian scriptures would consider self-forgiveness to be a form of blasphemy, putting oneself in the place of God. Besides, as many people have discovered, they cannot will their release from the spiritual prison that has been the result of their misbehavior. If people could forgive themselves, they would never have developed religious rituals that would help them experience the liberation that God alone can offer.

As people learn to accept God's offer of forgiveness, they often find the freedom to forgive other people. When people are obsessed by their shame and guilt, they are often afraid to forgive the people who have offended them. Having a low opinion of themselves, they attempt to bolster their self-esteem by savoring every hurt they have suffered. To forgive would be to give up their only way of claiming moral superiority and to be left with nothing but their own sense of unworthiness. The problem may be cumulative. I am especially aware of it when I talk with some elderly people. One widower, who lived alone, had few visitors, for reasons I soon came to understand. His business partner had cheated him; his wife had wasted his hard-earned money; his children had never shown any appreciation for all he had done for them; and he had forgiven none of them. He could not forgive them because he did not have an experience of being forgiven. If younger people could look ahead and picture the solitary confinement that they were preparing for their old age, they might be eager to hear that accepting God's forgiveness would give them the freedom to forgive other people and to remain connected to them.

In the paradoxical fashion that is typical of them, the gospels never quote Jesus as saying anything at all about asking other people to forgive you, but they all say Jesus taught that you should forgive other people. Both Matthew and Luke make absolute the command to forgive your sisters and brothers within the community (Matthew 18:21-22 and Luke 17:4). With our contemporary concepts of human relations, we might wonder how all this forgiving can go on if no one is asking to be forgiven. Although Luke assumes that the other person would know better than to ask you for forgiveness, the person who has sinned against you might say, "I repent," that is, "I have had a change of attitude." When you hear the word "repent," you must forgive.

According to Matthew, the necessity of forgiving is not simply a personal matter affecting individuals; it is the business of the community. Just before providing the absolute commandment to forgive, Matthew describes a three-step process by which the community can deal with a person who has offended someone:

> If another member of the church sins against you, go and point out the fault when the two of you are alone. If the member listens to you, you have regained that one. But if you are not listened to, take one or two others along with you, so that every word may be confirmed by the evidence of two or three witnesses. If the member refuses to listen to them, tell it to the church; and if the offender refuses to listen even to the church, let such a one be to you as a Gentile and a tax collector. (Matthew 18:15-17)

If you decide to let another person be like an alien or the despised agent of a foreign power occupying your country, how can you say that you have been willing to forgive? To forgive means literally to release. I wish that Jesus or the gospel writers had been more explicit on the subject, but apparently they thought that the kind of release that we human beings can grant each other is different from what God offers. Each of us has the power to lock other people out of our circle of concern, and we each have the power to let other people in. When we forgive, we release people from the emotional and spiritual exile to which we have consigned them, but if Matthew is right, we do not necessarily release them from geographic or economic banishment. For a community simultaneously to banish and to forgive offenders sounds tricky to me, but I cannot think of a better approach. The process provides the injured person a way to respond without becoming vindictive; it allows the community to uphold its standards of behavior; and it gives the offender a chance to hear the complaint and to be reconciled. The three-step formula together with the commandment to forgive also leaves the way open for the offender to return to the community. Since the offenders are already forgiven, they can come back to the community whenever they are willing to listen.

A community that helps people deal both with the results of their own faults and with the offenses they suffer at the hands of other people may have strong appeal even for the dubious and the skeptical. People without any religious convictions who feel trapped by guilt or shame may be ready to hear the gospel as a proclamation of freedom. They can claim their freedom when they are willing to undergo a change of attitude and to place their trust, not in other people or in themselves, but in God. Through the study of the Bible and through the rituals offered by the church, they can develop confidence in the gospel, God's willingness to set them free.

The Oppression of Fate

Perhaps nothing upsets some of us more than the random nature of evil. Whenever we hear that someone has lung cancer, we immediately want to know, did she smoke? If she did smoke, we can feel sorry for her, but relieved. We all quit smoking years ago; we are safe. But if she did not smoke, we feel a twinge of fear. Lung cancer could happen to any of us. Similarly, if we hear that someone we know was mugged, we want to know where it happened and at what time. If he was walking alone east of Twelfth Street in southeast Washington after eleven P.M., we feel distressed, but also a little smug. Because we would never behave so foolishly, we could not have such a threatening experience. If the mugging took place in broad daylight a block from where we live, our reaction is different.

The fear of becoming a random victim of either cancer or crime may uncover a deeper fear, a fear of death. Or perhaps it is not death that frightens us so much as the fear of being without control over our destinies. The major turnings of our lives may be subject to chance, to fate. Somehow, all of us must find a way of coming to terms with fate.

In our technological age, the most common way of dealing with fate involves looking for reasons, providing explanations, finding someone to blame. In other words, people cope with fate by denying the random nature of evil. After the death of their son in an automobile accident, the parents may want facts: was the driver of the truck that smashed into him sober? did the truck have a valid license and inspection sticker? what was the condition of the highway? how quickly did the ambulance arrive on the scene? They press for more and more information in the hope that by understanding exactly what happened and knowing who was at fault they will be able to live with the tragedy.

Others respond to fate with a shrug and a wan smile, saying, "Bad things happen." Or if they have recently read one of James Clavell's novels set in China or Japan, they might be inclined to say, "That's *joss*," or "That's *karma*." People who were brought up in the church might be displaying much the same attitude toward fate when they allow that what happened was "God's will." They may not mean that they actually believe that God is controlling all the circumstances of their lives, but that they are not going to worry about something beyond their control.

Although they do their best to deny the random nature of evil or to shrug off their fears, some people still feel oppressed by fate. Even if they wanted to, they could not follow Friedrich Nietzsche's dictum, *Amor fati,* "Love your fate." Fate all too often is totally unlovable. Fate is oppressive. When they are feeling oppressed by fate, some people may be ready to hear the gospel, the proclamation that they are free—free not from the workings of fate or from the randomness of evil, but from the oppression of fate. If they can hear the proclamation, they may learn that what weighs them down is not fate but the result of their trying to deny fate or to shrug off their concern.

Both denying and shrugging are attempts to find comfort by disengaging from reality. Both are methods we human beings have developed to deal with our feelings about tragic circumstances over which we have no control. They work like tranquilizers, dulling our perception of the anger and despair within us but doing nothing to change either the painful circumstances or our internal condition. People who cope with misfortune by dulling their senses often feel oppressed by life. When they become weary of the oppression, they may hear the promise of release in the gospel, but they may remain wary, realizing that the gospel demand for a change in attitude means that they will have to experience the feelings that they most dread.

Giving up the narcotic effects of denial and detachment can be as difficult as giving up cigarettes, perhaps more difficult. The promise of better physical health and longer life may have more appeal than the somewhat nebulous proposition that in facing reality you will feel less oppressed by fate. Besides, how can you have confidence in the gospel before you have any experience of the promised freedom? A person with an analytical sort of mind does not like to take propositions on faith.

A change of attitude and a trust in the gospel may be conceivable, however, for people who are willing to entertain the possibility that an unknown and unknowable sovereign rules the universe. Allowing oneself to imagine that God's realm includes the realities of every person's life calls for the kind of split-level thinking common among scientists, who on the one hand demand hard data while on the other speak of nature as if it were a manipulative and secretive being. In the great flood of 1993, when the Mississippi River and its tributaries overflowed the levees and dikes the Corps of Engineers had built at vast cost to protect farms and cities, the director of the Association of State Floodplain Managers reflected, "We've got to figure out some way to help people understand that Mother Nature will reclaim what's hers from time to time."[2] Skeptical people can learn to do the same sort of thinking about fate. At one level they can describe reality in terms of facts, and on another level they can picture ultimate reality as God, sovereign of heaven and earth.

An African American widow who is raising her three children with no help from anyone is determined they will have a better life than she has. She has a job and works hard. She keeps her children clean. She takes them to church. She reads to them when they are small and makes sure they do their homework when they are in school. Then her fourteen-year-old son gets hit by a stray bullet in a shoot-out between two drug gangs. He is dead by the time she gets to him.

If she has heard the gospel, how might she respond? She will not minimize the tragedy by calling it God's will, nor will she divert herself from her anger and despair by trying to find an explanation for the horror of her son's death. Instead, she will take her complaint directly to her sovereign and demand justice. If God reigns, then either God caused her son's death or God programmed random tragedy into creation. Either way God is responsible, and she has the right to demand an accounting. She has the right to direct her rage toward the source of her misery. I can imagine her demanding justice as she would from any human authority who has failed her: "You think this creation of yours is so wonderful. You come down here and try it. See what it's like to have your husband and son die, and to try to make it on your own. You see what it's like to live among people who quarrel and fight and oppress and kill each other. You see what it's like to be abused, scorned, and sometimes homeless. You see what it's like to die when you are full of the love of life. You see what it's like to call out in prayer and get no answer. You see what it's like to be a human being in this world you have made, and then maybe, just maybe, I'll forgive you."

For a time her rage may keep her afloat, but when the anger is exhausted, she will descend to the depths of her despair. There at last she may encounter the one to whom she had directed her complaint and realize that she carried in her heart the story of how long ago God had fulfilled her demand to see what it is like to suffer as a human being.

The freedom from the oppression of fate promised by the gospel includes the freedom to forgive God. We can forgive God, not for being limited or for giving us an incomplete creation, but for failing to deliver justice and for allowing us to be the victims of fate. We have an authority to whom we can direct our demands for justice, an authority who can forgive us, and an authority whom we can forgive. But if we are unwilling to hold God accountable for the universe, the gospel becomes an empty promise.

People who are willing to enter their despair and to forgive God often experience a rebirth of hope. By hope I do not mean a foolish optimism that everything will turn out for the best. Despair is like being confined to a room with no exit; hope is the discovery of a door standing open to the future. A picture of hope emerges in the

Revelation to St. John. When he has poured out his despair over the state of the church, he writes, "After this I looked, and there in heaven a door stood open!" Hope frequently arises out of despair because in despair people find a connection with all those other people who have similarly been wronged by fate, and they discover a connection with God, who became known in a particular way through a man's tragic death on a cross.

When people acknowledge the hope that arises within them, they are better equipped to handle the vicissitudes of fate than those who respond with detachment or denial. In turn, the church as a community can help create an atmosphere in which hope can prevail. It can encourage people to face their despair without evasion or equivocation and it can urge them to look toward the future with courage and confidence. On closer examination, an observer can discover that a Christian community being faithful to the Jesus of Nazareth story will always understand despair and hope to be inseparable. A community that knows the necessity of keeping hope alive will do everything possible to expose the despair that people are experiencing as they suffer from the inexorable machinations of fate.

People who want to accept both their despair and their hope can find in the church various kinds of help—counseling, Bible study, support groups, lectures—but perhaps the most important is ritual. A baptism can help parents acknowledge the sinking feeling in their hearts as they contemplate the terrible responsibility of rearing a child. A funeral can give those left behind permission to express their grief and anger when death came too soon. A wedding allows the father of the bride to act out his sense of loss and foreboding as he leaves his daughter at the altar. In each of these rites of passage, as the participants are invited to recognize their fear and despair, they are also directed toward the hope that will sustain them in the future. Through its ritual, the church regularly reminds its members that the gospel has granted them the freedom to live in hope because it has released them to enter the despair they experience when fate deals them another blow.

The Chaos of Emptiness

Thomas Naylor, an economist at Duke University, has written persuasively in *The Cold War Legacy* that the economic problems in the

United States and in the former Soviet Union have developed from the same cause: lack of meaning. Employees and owners alike find themselves engaged in meaningless endeavor. On the assembly line and in the manager's office, people put in their time without finding any ultimate purpose for what they do, while those who have no work find no meaning in their idleness. In addition to the personal toll of destructive behavior and breakup of families, this sense of meaninglessness also shows up in the form of a persistently sluggish economy and frequent outbreaks of chaos: industrial sabotage, employee pilfering, urban riots, and government corruption.

One way or another, every human being will find some way of making sense out of existence because no one can stay very long with a life that is completely empty, devoid of any meaning. Everybody has a religion. Not everybody engages in worship or has a clearly defined system of beliefs, but everybody finds a way to put meaning into life. Some people are astonished to discover that existence has no built-in meaning. People must construct meaning for themselves, using the materials at hand. The gospel proclaims that people have the freedom to be open about their search for meaning; the church exists to help them get on with their business of making sense out of nonsense in an aware and thoughtful way.

As a rule, most people with a history of skepticism about organized religion will not be open to hearing the gospel until a year or two has passed following some crisis that shattered the framework of meaning they had constructed for themselves. Sometimes the meaning is shattered by guilt, as it was for a woman who realized at her father's death that she had never told him how much she loved him and appreciated all he had sacrificed to put her through college and law school. After the funeral she could not help asking herself what was the meaning of her success, what was the point of her life. Meaning also can disappear when fate puts an end to an activity. A man in his early fifties who lived for his time on the tennis court and took pride in his superb physical condition fell off a ladder while reglazing a second-story window. He broke his left leg in eight places and will never walk normally again, let alone jog or play tennis. So now what would be the point of getting up in the morning, of eating and drinking and going to work? Either guilt or fate can make life seem formless or empty.

Some thoughtful people do not need an existential crisis to lose their sense of meaning. They can simply stop and analyze their lives—as many are inclined to do at a decade marker, a fortieth or fiftieth birthday—and decide that all their associations and activities and accomplishments add up to nothing. People who reach this point may feel locked in by a mortgage to pay and children to educate and become severely depressed. They may briefly contemplate suicide, but if life has no meaning, then it is highly unlikely that they would find meaning in death, so they put aside the idea of self-murder and grimly go on living. Or such a person may give up a lucrative public relations business along with a six-bedroom house and the hope of an Ivy League education for the children and move to a small sheep farm in Maine.

Or perhaps this will be the time for them to hear the gospel.

If people think the gospel will bring meaning to their lives, they have to learn quickly that it will also demand that they repent—specifically, that they change their attitude toward meaning. For a start, they will have to accept the premise with which the biblical approach to life begins: "In the beginning when God created the heavens and the earth, the earth was a formless void and darkness covered the face of the deep." The creation myth opens with the myth-makers' perception of reality, a formless void and chaos, for which "the deep" was their most vivid symbol. Then God spoke, and the word of God brought order and the possibility of life. Christians identify the word of God with Jesus of Nazareth: "The Word became flesh and lived among us." Because of their confidence in Jesus's message, they can admit that their existence appears to be empty and without form until they consciously or unconsciously invest their lives with purpose. Those who join them must be willing to make a similar admission if they are serious about their quest for meaning.

The early followers of Jesus seem to have been clear that what Jesus had to offer was not an answer to the question, "What is the meaning of my life?" Instead, what they found in the teachings of Jesus and in his story was encouragement as they searched for meaning. In describing why Jesus was important to them, they spoke not in terms of goals or of destinations but of "the way." The word they chose could mean a road, a highway, or a journey. In Jesus they had found a guide; in the church they had found companions for the journey they had undertaken when their old sense of order had collapsed.

People who have confidence in their guide and who have companions to join them on the way are free to create meaning for themselves as they go. A positive response to the gospel includes a willingness to invent meaning, with the understanding that the meaning invented may well be temporary and certainly will be fragile.

With Jesus as their guide, most people find more meaning in serving other people than they do in spending all their energy to further their personal interests. If the public relations consultant saw that he was genuinely helping both his clients and the public, and if he found time to volunteer his expertise to promote a tutoring program for inner-city children, he might not have to leave for Maine. If he did go to Maine and raise sheep, he would do so not just to find peace and quiet but also to provide a useful product and to help protect the environment from intensive development. With either choice, he would understand that either changing circumstances or deteriorating health could make the enterprise pointless.

The real problem with the meaning people create, even if they are Jesus followers, is that they tend to invest the meaning with more authority and certainty than it can bear. That is how practicing Christians on both sides of the abortion issue get into so much trouble. They have filled the empty places in their lives with a cause. If they are not careful, in time the cause defines them and their relationships with all other people. People who agree with them are good and righteous, and those who oppose them are wrong and deserve to be punished. They think of themselves as being above the law, answering only to a "higher law" that allows them to intrude on each other's meetings and to trespass on other people's property.

When a Christian community functions properly, however, its members can help each other test the meaning they have created for themselves. They can help each other avoid the trap of investing any source of meaning with ultimate authority and certainty and to look in new directions for meaning when an important source dries up. One community activist spent most of her free time for eleven years trying to thwart the state highway department's plan to put a six-lane expressway through her neighborhood. When the state legislature voted decisively to cancel the project, at first she was elated.

After the victory celebration, her elation quickly gave way to a feeling of emptiness. Without her church community to help her gain perspective, she easily could have become depressed. Through conversation with her friends at church, she realized that she had allowed the cause to become her savior, a substitute for God. Instead of becoming depressed, she chose to concentrate more consciously on her search for meaning.

Having a community makes such a positive difference as the search for meaning goes on that some people allow the church itself to provide the only form that keeps the chaos at bay. Such an attitude perverts the gospel and impedes evangelism among people who already suspect that the church has too much control over the lives of its members.

To remain faithful to the gospel and to be effective in evangelism, church members must constantly remind each other that the community is not the ultimate judge of how each person tries to fill the empty places in life. As church members reach out to new people, they must recognize among themselves that as they have become open about their search for meaning they have felt a growing desire for testing and judgment. They want to know how they are doing. Each is like a nine-year-old child who shows his art teacher a drawing in hope of praise but in fear of negative criticism. They must learn that no human institution can fulfill that need for judgment, but that the church may provide the occasion when people can become aware of God as their judge. Then they will know what the church has to offer those outsiders who have also become aware of their longing for a trustworthy evaluation of their attempts to find meaning. They will be in a position to help these new people understand that a positive response to the gospel includes a willingness to confess the desire for a judge who understands the desperation of their search for meaning and who knows the way.

Church members also must challenge any attempt to make belonging to the church a person's way of filling the void. The best way to create trouble for the future is to promise more than the church can provide. People who become upset and angry because the church has "failed" them are usually those who join with unrealistic expectations. If they think that somehow the church will be the answer to their problem of emptiness, or if they think that the church can be the meaning of their lives, they are likely to be disappointed. An even worse outcome than disappointment and an angry departure would be their continuing satisfaction with the church as their ultimate provider of belonging. Members who develop such an uncritical dependence on the church may seem to be an asset because they show up every time the church door is opened, but they become a drag on the energy and imagination of the community. They demand constant attention, especially from the clergy and the volunteer leaders. The best way to prevent either angry disappointment or unhealthy dependence begins with evangelism—letting prospective members know that the church will not fill their need to belong.

Before any congregation embarks on a campaign of evangelism, the members should have some idea of the *euangelion* they have to offer. If they hope to appeal to the dubious and the skeptical, they will need to find ways of discussing the gospel in plain English. My suggestions are just one way and are not likely to be the best in every situation, but I think that the members of any congregation interested in evangelism will be well-advised to adopt a similar discipline. When they need to use a metaphor or a split-level expression because plain English will not suffice, they will need to be clear with their listeners about what they are doing. In these conversations, what will matter the most will be their ability to describe the difference that Jesus's "proclamation of freedom" has made in their lives and in the lives of people they know. Preparing themselves to do their part in discussing the gospel may take some church members time and effort if they are not accustomed to thinking and talking about their faith in analytical terms.

Learning to talk about Jesus's message with people who have been put off by organized religion is only part of the preparation required. Another significant part of becoming equipped for evangelism is learning to talk about Jesus himself.

Chapter 7

What Can We Say About Jesus?

When I was growing up, I had the misfortune of following a brilliant older sister into the public school. Most of my teachers had taught my sister two years before they had me in class, and they found countless little ways to let me know that I did not measure up to the standard she had set and that I should try harder to be like her. I should show more imagination in my writing; I should be more accurate in my arithmetic; I should sing on key; I should be getting better grades. By the sixth grade I really thought that I hated my older sister. It was not until I finished college that I figured out she was not responsible for making me feel inadequate all through school. My antagonism toward her was my defense against the feelings that bubbled up in me every time a teacher held up my brilliant and highly competent older sister as an example for me to emulate.

In a similar fashion, many of the products of our Sunday schools grew up hating Jesus because what they were taught by their teachers made them feel hopelessly inadequate. Those with the strongest aversion to Jesus often prove to be the offspring of Christian parents who made them go to Sunday school. In class after class, their teachers held up Jesus as the example of what they should grow up to be. From what they heard, Jesus was nauseatingly good, not at all the sort of person they would want for a friend, let alone the sort of person they would aspire to be. By the time they were old enough to resist their parents' demands that they go to Sunday school, they hated Jesus in the same way they would hate anyone whom adults held up as an example for them to emulate.

Evangelists who seek out the doubtful and skeptical cannot mention Jesus without risking a strong negative response, but neither can they ignore the subject. Because Jesus is at the center of the church's rituals, Christians must find ways of reintroducing the Jesus of the gospels to people who harbor strong negative feelings about him. One way to begin a conversation with the dubious and the skeptical about Jesus is to say, "Instead of spending his time with religious types, Jesus seemed to prefer the company of people like you, people who did not have much faith."

Jesus and His Friends of Little Faith

In the Gospel according to St. Matthew, Jesus has an affectionate name for his disciples, *oligopistoi*. The first half of the term means a little, or a few, as in "oligarchy," the rule of a few people or a small group, while the second comes from *pistis*, the familiar term for trust, confidence, belief, or faith. So Jesus is calling his closest associates people of little faith, or people with few beliefs. In some passages, it is possible to conclude that Matthew meant the reader to understand the term as an insult, or at least a rebuke, but that does not seem to be the case when Jesus first uses this name in addressing his disciples. He is nearing the end of a long discourse, known as the Sermon on the Mount, when he poses a rhetorical question: "If God so clothes the grass of the field, which is alive today and tomorrow is thrown into the oven, will he not much more clothe you—you of little faith?" At this point in the story, the disciples were just standing or sitting around listening to Jesus. They were doing nothing that could have prompted Jesus to use a derogatory term in speaking directly to them. From the context, Jesus's name for his followers as a group seems to have been one of familiarity if not genuine affection. He apparently liked people for whom doubt was a more characteristic response than faith.

Oligopistoi has a kind of teasing or bantering quality that Jesus reserves for his most intimate associates. In Matthew's gospel, Jesus does identify at least two people as having great faith. Both of them are outsiders, and both immediately disappear from the story, never to be heard from again. One of them is a Canaanite woman who pesters Jesus to heal her daughter, and the other is a Roman centurion who insists that Jesus can heal his slave without even going to see him. Jesus commends them for their faith, but as far as the story goes, neither of them became followers.

Once we realize that Jesus calls no one but his followers "you of little faith," the designation has a different sound in the stories where Jesus is reprimanding them. In one of these stories, a sudden storm catches Jesus and his disciples out in a boat on the Sea of Galilee. Even though waves are swamping the boat, Jesus sleeps soundly until his disciples wake him up, pleading, "Lord, save us." Their behavior might not seem odd until you recall that the disciples were experienced fishermen who had spent their working lives on the sea, and that Jesus was the only landlubber in the boat. His response betrays a little annoyance at having his sleep interrupted by men who knew a good deal more about sailing than he did: "Why are you afraid, you of little faith?" In the context of Jesus's developing relationship with his disciples, his question sounds more like teasing than scolding. What could be sillier than sailors asking a carpenter what to do about a boat during a storm at sea?

The other time Jesus calls the whole group "you of little faith" occurs in a story that can be useful in talking about Jesus with people who do not think of themselves as believers. On this occasion, just as the disciples catch up with Jesus, who had crossed the Sea of Galilee ahead of them, they realize that they have forgotten to bring any bread. Ignoring their predicament, Jesus tells them to beware of the yeast of the Pharisees and Sadducees. Apparently confused, the disciples wonder if Jesus is talking about the forgotten bread. Then Jesus says to them: "You of little faith, why are you talking about having no bread? Do you still not perceive?" He appears to be irritated because the disciples fail to understand that he is speaking in metaphors and not referring to the fact that they forgot bring any bread to eat on another boat trip. People of little faith need constant reminding that they are not to take religious teaching literally but to look for the symbolic meaning, but they can learn. In fact, Matthew seems to suggest that the people of little faith are the only ones worth teaching.

Matthew confirms this view in the only story in which Jesus honors a single individual with the title. He is none other than Peter, the disciple Matthew considers to be the leader of the community after the death of Jesus. The story is of Peter's failed attempt to imitate Jesus by walking on water. As he is about to sink, Jesus offers him a hand, and addresses him by what we have now seen is a term of real affection: "You of little faith, why did you doubt?" The story reflects what Jesus stands for in human experience. Some people occasionally experience a momentary sense of confidence, which is another word for faith; they take an uncharacteristic risk; they fail, but they are ready to try again. Jesus chose his followers from the ranks of those with inconsistent, faltering, periodic faith, not those whose faith was sure and steady. When those people were willing to act on what little faith they had, he was willing to lend a hand if they needed him.

Although Luke has Jesus call his disciples "you of little faith" only once—in the passage where Jesus is telling them not to worry about their lives, what they are to eat or what they are to wear—Luke seems to have the same attitude toward faith among the disciples that we have seen in Matthew. Luke's opinion of faith comes through in a story that he alone relates. The disciples make what seems to be a reasonable request, "Increase our faith!" It is a request that many people both in and outside the church might make, because people who cannot believe easily often look wistfully at people with faith. If they knew how to acquire more faith, they would get it. The request of the disciples was reasonable because they knew that faith was a gift from God, but Jesus's response was hardly sympathetic. It might even have been a bit unkind: "If you had faith the size of a mustard seed, you could say to this mulberry tree, 'Be uprooted and planted in the sea,' and it would obey you."

This saying has always attracted me. The neighborhood where I live in Washington, D.C., has a great many mulberry trees because of a misguided attempt to raise silkworms in the nineteenth century. The silkworms did not last long, but the mulberry trees that were planted to feed them not only flourished but spread through an entire section of the city and are a real nuisance. We have one in the backyard, and I have often thought it would be a fine thing to walk out one morning and say to the mulberry tree, "Be uprooted and planted in the sea!" It would be like a documentary I once saw about the launching of the space shuttle from Cape Canaveral: a great rumbling and roaring and a cloud of dust as the huge mulberry tree rises up and gains speed as it arches over Lincoln Park, adjusts its course, and heads out over Chesapeake Bay.

The reader of Luke's story must ask, "Was Jesus being serious?" If it only took a little bit of faith, a bit so small you could hardly see it, to uproot mulberry trees and cast them into the Sea of Galilee, think what mischief people could do if they had great faith. I do not think Luke wanted the reader to think that Jesus intended his words to be taken at face value, but to reveal to the disciples that they had made a silly request. Instead of telling them that they had made a silly request, he gave them a silly answer. To make sure that the disciples did not misunderstand, Luke says Jesus went on to suggest that asking for more faith is as foolish as a slave expecting that his master will ask him to sit at the table and have dinner before the master and the family have eaten. Everybody knows that even though a slave may have put in a full day's work in the field he will have to serve the master and the family before he can eat. To expect life to be otherwise would be ridiculous.

Then Luke moves on to other matters without bothering to relate how the disciples reacted, but I imagine they would have been disappointed and that their disappointment might have turned to anger. I think they developed an appreciation for what he had given them only after his death. Jesus had suggested that they did not need more faith, for they had all the faith they could ever use, all the faith they needed to face life and death. If they had any more faith, they might do something dangerous, such as uprooting mulberry trees and sending them flying to the sea.

The attitude toward faith that Jesus exemplified might open up conversations with people who do not think they belong in church because they think their faith is inadequate. Jesus can become a much more attractive figure to alienated people when they discover that Jesus did not care to spend much time with people of great faith but instead surrounded himself with those of little faith. He was so fond of little faith people that he discouraged them from trying to acquire more faith. At least that is the way the gospels according to Matthew and Luke present Jesus. Evangelists who want to reintroduce outsiders to Jesus can take their cues from these two

gospels and present Jesus as a friend to those who do
faith.

Jesus as Teacher

Questioning people who have avoided Jesus because h   ins to
represent the irrational and mindless aspects of faith also may
change their minds when they discover he was something like them.
As the gospels remember Jesus, he never asked people to accept
what he said on faith. In a variety of ways, Jesus insisted that people
think for themselves.

For one thing, Jesus never gave a straight answer to a simple
question. Following the great intellectual tradition of Judaism, he always responded to a question by turning the question back on the
person who asked it, and often he responded to a question with another question. A lawyer asked Jesus, "Teacher, what must I do to in-
herit eternal life?" He answered him, "What is written in the law?
What do you read there?" Another time someone in the crowd said
to Jesus, "Teacher, tell my brother to divide the family inheritance
with me." His response was, "Friend, who set me to be a judge or ar-
bitrator over you?"

Another technique Jesus used in trying to get people to think was
to respond to their questions with puzzling stories. For example, the
lawyer who asked Jesus the question about eternal life answered the
question Jesus posed him by quoting two verses from the Torah:
"You shall love the Lord your God with all your heart, and with all
your soul, and with all your strength, and with all your mind; and
your neighbor as yourself." Jesus commended him for his answer,
but the lawyer was not willing to let the matter rest. He asked a second question, "And who is my neighbor?" Jesus replied with the
story of the Good Samaritan and yet another question.

Look at the story in Luke 10:29-36. It is in no way responsive to
the question posed by the lawyer, and it is not a pious reflection. It is
a story that raises questions: about the dangers of traveling alone,
about the integrity of those who represent organized religion, about
the prejudice of Jews toward Samaritans, about the financial responsibility of a traveler who happens to come across the victim of a vio-
lent crime. Every one of these implicit questions contains a moral
dilemma worth pondering. How much should I be concerned about

my personal safety? How far should I trust religious leaders to set standards for me? How hard should I try to make contact with people of other ethnic groups? How great an effort should I make to help a stranger in trouble? Telling puzzling stories was one method Jesus used to make people think.

Whether all the stories Jesus told were responses to questions no one can say, but we can say that he probably told these stories, known as parables, to make people think. Unfortunately, when Christianity moved out of the peasant culture of Palestine to the cities of the Greek and Roman world, the new members of the church from urban cultures did not understand Jesus's method of teaching and tried to make sense of the parables by treating them as allegories. While a parable sets a whole story alongside reality, an allegory presents characters and events that parallel actual situations. For centuries Christians employed an allegorical interpretation to the parables, but with the advent of the critical approach to the texts, scholars came to the conclusion that the "parable had not the carefully constructed detail of an allegory."[1] Teachers or preachers in the western world use allegories to make their points, but as Kenneth Bailey pointed out in his book *Through Peasant Eyes,* Jesus taught in a typical oriental fashion using a "dramatic form of theological language that presses the listener to respond."[2] In other words, the parables of Jesus do not answer questions but provoke the listener or reader to a deeper level of questioning. Looking for the questions, by the way, is an exercise that can appeal to people who are more interested in analyzing than in coming up with definitive answers.

As the gospels present Jesus, even when his life was threatened he refused to give a direct answer to a straight question. According to Luke, on the morning after Jesus was arrested, he was brought before the assembly of elders, which included both priests from the temple and scribes, those learned in the law. All of them asked, "Are you, then, the Son of God?" He answered, "You say that I am." Of course, the elders had said no such thing. They had asked him a question that he was refusing to answer, but Luke in telling the story about the elders' interrogation of Jesus is using the same method he attributes to Jesus. At this critical point in the drama, he is posing a question for the reader. Who is this Jesus? Jesus himself would never say. Now all people who hear the story must come to their own conclusions and decide who Jesus will be for them.

Even when Jesus was not posing questions or telling puzzling stories, he was encouraging people to think for themselves. One device he used was the aphorism, which the dictionary defines as a terse saying that embodies a general truth or astute observation. Clifton Fadiman once wrote that an aphorism contains "only as much wisdom as an overstatement will permit." A capable aphorist can undermine conventional wisdom by overstating the case in a way that both amuses people and makes them think, and Jesus was one of these.

The collection of sayings known as the Beatitudes provides good examples of the aphorism. Each statement begins with the plural form of *makarios,* an adjective that is usually translated "blessed." It suggests that fate or the gods were smiling on a person; it means fortunate, lucky, or happy in the original meaning of the word. Happiness is so often associated with a feeling that people forget its connection to per*hap*s and to *hap*pen, but *hap* means chance or luck. A person who could be called *makarios* was one who had already found good fortune, or rather one whom good fortune had found.

To appreciate the aphoristic nature of Jesus's teaching, just look down Matthew's list of lucky people. Among the fortunate people listed are the poor, those who mourn, the meek, the hungry and thirsty, and those who are persecuted, reviled, and have lies told about them. Most scholars think that if Jesus said these things, he did not say them all at once.[3] Matthew probably has collected a series of statements that Jesus originally delivered as one-liners, each one intended to startle his audience. How could anyone with the least bit of common sense equate poverty, grief, submissiveness, famine, and persecution with good luck?

From a strictly logical perspective, Jesus's one-liners make no sense, but they can challenge you to question truths that you have always taken for granted. If you are willing to stop and think about what Jesus said, you may discover that each of the Beatitudes contains all the wisdom that an overstatement will permit. Perhaps those who are poor enough to beg are lucky in that they know what they need; if theirs is a poverty of the spirit, they are lucky that at least they know what they are missing. Perhaps people who mourn are luckier than those who cannot allow themselves to grieve; often people in grief form connections that were impossible when everyone seemed to be cheerful. Perhaps you are lucky if you do not have to walk all over other people to convince yourself that you matter; only people with a high degree of self-esteem can afford to be humble. Perhaps people are lucky if they realize that they live in a time of ethical famine, when justice is hard to find; if they know how much they hunger and thirst for righteousness, they might find ways to create a more just society. Perhaps people who are persecuted are luckier than those who are most admired and applauded; at least they have their feet on the ground and have the satisfaction of knowing that they are engaged in an important struggle. Perhaps even the merciful, the pure in heart, and the peacemakers are lucky; they do not need admiration and respect to work at making this a better world. Whether or not you agree that Jesus's overstatements contain some wisdom, you may find that his aphorisms have given people with a questioning attitude something worth pondering.

According to Matthew, besides using aphorisms Jesus also undermined conventional thought by urging people to challenge contemporary interpretations of ancient wisdom. In a compilation of Jesus's teachings that follow the Beatitudes, he introduces a formula:

> You have heard that it was said to those of ancient times, "You shall not murder"; and "whoever murders shall be liable to judgment." But I say to you that if you are angry with a brother or sister, you will be liable to judgment; and if you insult a brother or sister, you will be liable to the council; and if you say, "You fool," you will be liable to the hell of fire. (Matthew 5:21-22)

By using this formula ("You have heard that it was said...But I say to you..."), he opens up questions in other areas that his listeners might have thought were settled, questions about sex, oaths, retaliation, and love. Matthew did not think Jesus was repudiating the ancient wisdom, only questioning how people were using their tradition. He reports that Jesus said, "Do not think that I have come to abolish the law or the prophets; I have come not to abolish but to fulfill." His method of fulfilling the Jewish heritage was to push each ethical principle to the point at which no one could claim perfect righteousness. He also looked behind destructive behavior to the attitude that produced the unlawful act and warned against the attitude. Anger and cursing often precede murder; looking at another for the purpose of sexual excitement can lead to adultery. By challenging the way people were accustomed to think about moral principles, Jesus was getting people to entertain disturbing thoughts about themselves. If they thought they were righteous because they had never killed anybody or committed adultery, they may have missed the point of the Torah and the warnings of the prophets, and they may have put themselves in an ethically precarious position.

What Jesus said about the Torah and the prophets can guide evangelists for a comprehensive church. By imitating the approach Jesus took toward his tradition, we can show outsiders that we support their questioning of conventional Christianity. As we try to present Jesus in a favorable light to people who are skeptical about organized religion, we also can show conventional Christians that we have not come to abolish Christianity but to help fulfill its promise. We have no quarrel with our biblical tradition, but we want to challenge the way people have been interpreting the wisdom we have inherited from the past.

The Skepticism of Jesus

The gospel writers and editors may have been saying as much about themselves as they were about Jesus when they portrayed the skeptical side of his nature, but they have provided an invaluable service for anyone who is introducing Jesus to a skeptical audience. Luke's gospel claims that Jesus began questioning religious authorities when he was only twelve years old, and all four gospels repeatedly speak of his disputes with both priests and scholars. Some Christians like to think that Jesus was primarily interested in pointing out the flaws and weaknesses of Judaism, but I think it is more accurate to say that Jesus was skeptical of organized religion. He had the same kinds of questions about the religious teachings and practices of his day that many skeptics today have about Christianity. He questioned the value of tithing for people who "have neglected the weightier matters of the law: justice and mercy and faith" as much as he objected to displays of piety, praying in public and making a show of contributing to charity. He challenged the strict application of rules and regulations without regard for changing circumstances

(Matthew 23:13-15) and complained about the extent to which missionaries would go to make a convert without ever stopping to examine their own relationship to God (Matthew 23:23).

Jesus displayed his skepticism not only by what he taught but also by what he did with institutional religion. Luke tells a story about the trouble he stirred up in his hometown synagogue. Not long after Jesus began his career as an itinerant teacher, he went back to Nazareth. The leaders of the synagogue were obviously glad to see him; they invited him to read from one of the ancient writings and to comment on what he had read. At first people seemed pleased with this native son who had returned home: "All spoke well of him and were amazed at the gracious words that came from his mouth." Then, after questioning the sincerity of their praise, Jesus began to challenge them with familiar stories from Scripture:

> The truth is, there were many widows in Israel in the time of Elijah, when the heaven was shut up three years and six months, and there was a severe famine over all the land; yet Elijah was sent to none of them except to a widow at Zarephath in Sidon. There were also many lepers in Israel in the time of the prophet Elisha, and none of them was cleansed except Naaman the Syrian. (Luke 4:25-27)

When the good people of Nazareth heard this, they were filled with rage. Apparently they did not like to be reminded that part of the reason they enjoyed going to religious gatherings was that the practice made them feel superior to all those poor, benighted souls who were not of the right sort. Jesus's suggestion that God might love foreigners more than God loved them was so offensive that they wanted to kill him. Jesus's skepticism about the Jewish claims of superiority was similar to the skepticism many outsiders today display toward the Christians' assumption of their superiority over all other religious traditions.

Just as Jesus questioned the attitudes he found in the local congregation, he raised objections to practices he found at the temple in Jerusalem. All four of the gospels tell the story of Jesus overturning the tables of the moneychangers and driving out the people who sold animals for the ritual sacrifices. His objection seems to have been that the business of the temple had become business; according to John, he warned them, "Stop making my Father's house a marketplace!" I hear the same sort of complaint about the church. People doubt the usefulness of a religious institution whose energies become absorbed by its need for money. That charge in our day, as in the time of Jesus, is more frequently leveled at national organizations than at local congregations. Supporting the headquarters building and the bureaucrats who staff it can become an end in itself, as was the case with the Jerusalem temple and its priests and Levites.

The way Matthew and Mark tell his story, the skepticism of Jesus was not limited to religious institutions and their teaching. He also had his doubts about God. When he was in agony on the cross, Jesus cried with a loud voice, "My God, my God, why have you forsaken me?" That is a skeptic's prayer, a prayer addressed to the absent God. Many people outside the church say that they believe in some sort of God, but doubt if God looks after them. When they get into deep distress, God does not seem to be around. These two gospels suggest that Jesus had a similar experience. I realize, of course, that the cry of despair attributed to Jesus is also the first line of the twenty-second psalm, a poem that closes with a ringing affirmation of faith. I suppose it is possible that Matthew and Mark wanted their readers to think that Jesus had the entire psalm in mind but only had the strength to recite the opening verse, but since we have no evidence to substantiate that speculation, I think anyone can feel free to use the story as it stands in reintroducing Jesus to people who doubt God's interest in them.

Jesus as the Son of God

Although the contemporary evangelist can reintroduce Jesus as a friend of those with little faith and as a person who had his own skeptical attitudes, the potential recruit may still offer the objection: "I can't be a Christian because I don't believe in the divinity of Jesus," or "I don't believe that Jesus was the *only* son of God." They resent the words attributed to Jesus: "No one comes to the Father except through me." These objections go to the heart of the resistance to Christianity because of its claims of an access to God that is exclusive, or at least superior to what other religions can provide. Once again, the evangelist's best resource for meeting the problem turns out to be the Bible. In talking to those who have serious questions about the link between Jesus and God, the evangelist would do well to dig behind doctrines and creeds to find what the first followers of Jesus may have meant when they said, "For God so loved the world that he gave his only Son, so that everyone who believes in him may not perish but may have eternal life."

For a start, the evangelist can point out that, with the exception of the Gospel according to St. John and the First Letter of John, the New Testament does not call Jesus the *only* son of God, and that John's gospel begins by asserting the potential of all people to be children of God. If John thought that all could be children of God, he could not have used "only" in the sense of "no other" but must have meant what we mean by "unique." As a child of God, Jesus was unique in the eyes of his followers. They found in him something that they did not find in other people, something that caused them to use in a special way the common metaphor "son." Any "son of" metaphor suggests that the person so named has particular attributes, either admirable or detestable, as when Jesus called the brothers James and John "sons of thunder." When the disciples called Jesus a son of God, they probably intended to convey something more than their observation that Jesus possessed the divine qualities of love and wisdom. When they called Jesus the son of God, they seem to have been saying that through Jesus they had found a new connection to God or a new understanding of God. As theologian Paul van Buren has stressed, "The Apostolic Writings nowhere clearly call Jesus God, yet it can be said that the story of Jesus is told as the story of God."[4]

The first followers of Jesus had a difficult time describing just what impact Jesus continued to have on their lives. When ordinary language failed them, they used the special language of religious experience. For example, consider an episode known as the transfiguration, which appears in three of the gospels. Matthew calls the experience of the disciples a "vision," which in the Bible always refers to a moment of insight, either sleeping or waking. In the story of the transfiguration, the three people closest to Jesus—Peter and the brothers James and John—are with Jesus on a mountain top when they have a vision of him talking with Moses and Elijah. In the vision, Jesus is transfigured, that is he is changed from his ordinary appearance to a dazzling figure radiating light. Then after Moses and Elijah appear and talk with him, a bright cloud covers the mountain, and from the cloud a voice says, "This is my son."

The vivid imagery used to describe the vision points to a profound experience that took place when the disciples were filled with both hope and fear. Jesus had decided to leave the familiar territory of Galilee and to confront the authorities in Jerusalem. The mission had the possibility of producing a religious awakening among the Jewish people, but the Romans might perceive his presence in the provincial capital as a threat to civil order. The disciples had tried to talk him out of such a dangerous move, but once he had made up his mind, they had decided to go with him. They had been living with considerable stress as they drew closer to Jerusalem so his three friends could have welcomed Jesus's invitation to take time away by themselves on the mountain. Any reader can easily understand why their first response to the vision was to linger on the mountain. They offered to build three temporary shelters, such as farmers from the villages made when they could not take time to go home at night during harvest time. They wanted to keep that sense of being with Jesus, Moses, and Elijah.

The bright cloud that covered them suggests both the intensity and the personal quality of the vision. I have spent many summers in a mountaintop village that is frequently covered by clouds. Under certain conditions, the cloud can be dazzlingly bright while visibility is limited to about twenty-five or thirty yards. With the rest of the world shut out, any given space inside the cloud can be intensely private. In the story, Jesus reinforces that sense of the vision being a personal matter by telling the disciples to tell no one about the vision. Other people could easily misunderstand what the vision meant to them. They could become fascinated by the details of the vision itself rather than the insight the vision was meant to convey.

The vision points directly to what the followers of Jesus had in mind when they called him God's son. To them, he was of the same stature as Moses and Elijah. Like his two predecessors, Jesus was a prophet. In ancient times, when the people of Israel had listened to the prophetic voices of Moses and Elijah, they had felt the presence of the LORD—the God of Abraham, Isaac, and Jacob; the God of Sarah, Deborah, and Ruth. In much the same way, the disciples of Jesus realized that when they listened to him, they seemed to be in the presence of the God whom their people had always worshiped. The people who heard the disciples' stories about Jesus had a similar experience of God's presence with them. They became followers of Jesus because Jesus provided a connection with God.

For the people who wrote and circulated the gospels, Jesus was God's special representative. In their minds, Jesus was almost an extension of God—like a merchant's son who could be his father's agent, knowing the mind of his father and representing his father's interests. When some of them called Jesus "God's only son," they were not making a statement about the nature of God so much as they were trying to express what Jesus meant to them. For them, Jesus provided a unique opportunity to feel connected with God. The followers of Jesus who wrote and edited the gospels wanted other people to have the same opportunity to know the presence of God through the teachings of Jesus and the stories about Jesus.

People who have serious questions about Jesus can stay with their questions and still become faithful members of a church that assembles in his name if the church does not expect more of them than the gospel writers and editors expected of their first readers. People with doubts and skepticism about the role of Jesus in the great scheme of the cosmos can practice Christianity with integrity if they can accept the language used about Jesus in the spirit in which it was probably first written. If they understand that the traditional symbols associated with the name of Jesus point to an internal experience and not just an external reality, they will be open to the same possibility of knowing the presence of God that was available to those who listened to Moses and to Elijah and to Jesus of Nazareth.

Part Three

Chapter 8

Creating a Climate for Growth

Although successful evangelism of any kind requires careful planning and bold action, nothing much will be possible until the leaders of the congregation start concentrating on the religious atmosphere in their own church. In countless subtle ways—from the signs on the doors to the way members interact with one another—the congregation is constantly putting out messages that reveal who is welcome and who is not. Both current members and those who drop in receive these messages, and both respond to what they hear. If the tenor of parish life is marked primarily by the desire for exclusive membership, the leadership of the church will need to spend a considerable amount of time working to promote a more inclusive atmosphere. Unless clergy and volunteer parish leaders pay close attention to the atmosphere in which they intend to establish a new approach to expanding their membership, they will have no hope of success. Before concentrating on the many details that contribute to the climate of parish life, the church leaders committed to the kind of evangelism that makes room for doubt and skepticism might want to start with major areas over which they have primary influence.

Any changes in the climate of parish life will also require a high degree of cooperation between the clergy and the lay leaders. Clergy often find themselves to be poorly prepared for the new kinds of behavior called for in a genuinely open church, and yet they must play a pivotal role. Unless they have the support of the elected and appointed leaders of their congregations when they are under stress, the clergy probably will revert to the behavior they learned at home and in seminary. When they are anxious, clergy are often in danger of becoming arbitrary and authoritarian, traits that have a way of limiting discussion and stifling questions. They can handle their anxiety in more creative ways when they are confident that the lay leaders are behind them.

Permission to Argue

No single factor contributes as much to the climate of parish life as the leadership's way of dealing with differences of opinion. As church leaders look for ways to encourage questioning and express doubt, they would do well to keep in mind the prophet Isaiah's word to Israel after disastrous domestic and foreign policies had left the country in ruins: "Come, let us argue it out" (Isaiah 1:18). "Argue" is the word used in the New Revised Standard Version. Older translations sound much more genteel—"Come, let us reason together"— but obscure the imagery of the law court that Isaiah was evoking. Permission to argue is essential in creating the atmosphere that will appeal to people who have an analytical mind-set, but many church people have trouble accepting the permission. Their fathers had intervened in disputes with the firm admonishment, "Don't argue with your mother." Their grandmothers had told them, "If you can't say anything nice, don't say anything at all." The only exception to the no-arguing rule occurred in the courts of law. Arguing in any other place was impolite. They learned to use their best manners with God and in God's house, and that meant absolutely no arguments in church or in private prayer.

The no-arguing rule may have provided some much appreciated peace and quiet for harried parents and exasperated clergy, but the side effects have been disastrous. Conversations in families and among church people have been reduced to discussions of the weather and of football scores, while disputes bubble along just under the surface. A sixty-year-old man is estranged from his older sister because he still resents her playing the radio while he was trying to do his high school homework. Three families maintain their membership in the church with small annual contributions but seldom attend services because they are still angry about the amount of money the congregation spent renovating the parsonage ten years ago. Among the people who attended church when they were young and do so no longer are those with resentments that they buried because they could not argue with the adults in the congregation or with God.

Church leaders can teach the congregation the importance of arguing things out by referring them to the Bible in sermons or study groups; even more effective is the introduction of Bible study into committee meetings or conferences for parish planning. In time, most of the congregation can learn that, beginning with Adam, the Bible tells stories about people arguing with God. Abraham tries to convince God that Sodom and Gomorrah are worth saving. Jeremiah does his best to persuade God to intervene in the affairs of Judah by punishing the wicked. Jesus argues constantly with his detractors as well as his followers. Paul's letters show him to be engaged in running arguments with people in the congregations he established.

The real change in a congregation's attitude toward arguing, however, will come through practice. With practice, people can learn how to argue with each other and with God. They can learn to argue and stay connected, not superficially—as they would if everyone were being polite—but solidly, in a way that is possible only among those who respect their differences. Usually the best opportunity for practice in arguing is when the parish faces a major decision, such as undertaking a major building program. All too often when serious differences of opinion arise in the congregation over such matters, the members spend most of their time talking with those who agree with them and becoming angry with people on the other side.

To create a healthy argument, the leaders can gather the congregation at an early stage and invite them to examine the issue by stating both sides of the impending decision and by identifying all the possible consequences of action or inaction. That is, the leaders arbitrarily assign people to participate in groups, each group having one of four possible assignments: (1) List all of the things you like about the building the way it is; (2) List all of the advantages you can think of that might come with a major renovation; (3) List the problems that a building renovation could cause; (4) List the problems that the congregation will live with if they do not renovate the building. No matter what their personal feelings about the situation, people in groups with assignments 1 and 3 will be developing arguments against the renovation, and those with assignments 2 and 4 in favor of it. This arrangement gets all the legitimate arguments out on the table without pushing the congregation into hostile camps. By using all four quadrants, the church can steer clear of the simple "pro versus con" debate that leads to polarization. Those who have already made up their minds are given an opportunity to look at the costs of getting their way. This approach to decision-making also lets people of every shade of opinion know that the rest of the congregation can respect their position no matter what the final decision.

As people learn to argue with each other on an institutional level, they also need encouragement to argue with each other face to face. Our own congregation requires that all people who become confirmed communicants of the parish promise to take both their praise and their complaints directly to the people involved. Although direct praise seldom sparks an argument, the act of expressing appreciation directly provides practice in straightforward communication that will make arguing seem more natural. I cannot boast that people in the congregation never talk about a person who is not present, but if the praising or complaining becomes excessive, someone probably will ask the question, "Have you told this person how you feel?" The standard is clear. No one is to deliver a message in order to save a person from the discomfort of telling the truth directly.

Incidentally, the standard of directing expressions of complaint or of praise to the appropriate person protects the clergy from becoming the recipients of everyone's anger and increases the possibility that those who do well will receive thanks. "You couldn't find any cream for the coffee this morning? Tell the person who chairs the hospitality committee." "You particularly enjoyed the anthem? I hope you told the director of music." In some congregations the tendency to bring up with the clergy matters that are not really their business is matched by the probability that no one will question them in an area that is their business. People who have trouble speaking to authority figures about what is on their minds need encouragement if they are going to tell their clergy what they really think. Congregations can provide that encouragement by instituting a program that gives church members a chance to talk back to their preachers.

Interactive Preaching

People may be entertained or bored by preaching; they may be enlightened or confused; but they seldom say anything more than "Nice sermon." A bland, unchallenging response to preaching contributes more than most people realize to an oppressive atmosphere in church, especially if the sermons themselves leave no room for asking questions. The economist Thomas Naylor suggests that much preaching seems to be aimed at the people who are comfortable with their beliefs while ignoring those who are actively engaged in the search for meaning:

> By playing to the segment of the congregation which has for the most part long since abandoned the search, ministers, priests, and rabbis drive away many thoughtful people who are turned off by unsubstantiated promises. These are the very people who are capable of giving religious institutions new vision and much needed energy.[1]

Clergy who want to provide visitors with something more thought-provoking may do their best to adopt a more open style that invites questions, but this is difficult to accomplish alone. If they are serious about wanting to broaden their appeal, they can arrange for their sermons to become more interactive by inviting groups of parishioners to join them in the preparation of sermons. The sermon planning group can study the assigned Bible passages with the preacher and identify the questions that the texts provoke about their heritage and about their lives.

One such group was studying a lesson from the last chapter of the Gospel according to St. John, a passage that ends, "This was now the third time that Jesus appeared to the disciples after he was raised from the dead." One of the first people to speak wondered why the author staged three resurrection appearances, each of which conveys the same message: death could not negate the meaning of Jesus's life and teaching. "What was John getting at? Does he want us to think the disciples didn't get it the first two times?" From there the conversation moved on to a consideration of how hard it is to learn anything the first time around, especially if you are depressed, as the disciples must have been following Jesus's death. As individuals, most of us realize we have had to learn over and over that new life can follow the facing of unpleasant truths. But why is it that we as a society can never seem to learn? Didn't the authorities in Los Angeles know that in having the police who beat Rodney King tried by an all-white suburban jury they were inviting the riot that left forty-four people dead? These questions formed the heart of the sermon, a sermon that concluded with the possibility that John was telling his readers that God may be like mothers or fathers who do not give up on their children even when they do not seem to learn.

At the very least, this process of sermon preparation will help the preacher avoid the common criticism that sermons seem to provide answers to questions that nobody is asking. When the sermon planning system works best, the volunteers receive the encouragement that comes from having their doubts and uncertainties respected and addressed by the person in the pulpit.

Sermon planning groups also can be helpful in reminding preachers about how certain Bible passages sound in the ears of people in the pews as opposed to how they strike a person who has been immersed in the study of Scripture for years. One group that was working on Matthew's parable of the sheep and the goats wanted to talk about their feelings of individual guilt for failing to do enough for the poor, the homeless, and the hungry. But the preacher came with a different reaction. He was prepared to discuss collective responsibility because he understood that the passage begins with the announcement: "All the *nations* will be gathered before (the Son of Man), and he will separate people one from another as a shepherd separates the sheep from the goats." The preacher knew that the original text does not include the word "people." It says simply that those to be separated are "them," a pronoun for which the only possible antecedent is "the nations." In a few minutes, the preacher learned that if he tried to preach about collective responsibility while individuals in the congregation were wrapped up in a consideration of personal guilt, no one would hear what he had to say. The sermon would somehow have to address the question of individual guilt aroused by the passage before putting the verse into its appropriate context. As representatives of their fellow parishioners, the volunteers in such a group can keep the preacher engaged in a genuine dialogue between pew and pulpit.

To maintain the interactive quality of preaching, the clergy can invite the group that helped prepare the sermon, or another group, to critique the results. One simple device for a critique is simply listing in two columns the group's responses to the questions, "Where did the sermon hit the mark for you? Where did it miss?" If people in the group are honest, this can be a difficult exercise for the preacher. I can still recall the feelings I had when one person in the critique group ignored the lists and said, "On a ten point scale, that sermon was about a four point five." If preachers can keep quiet and listen, they will not only be encouraging people to be forthright in challenging authority, they also may learn something about their preaching that will be helpful the next time in the pulpit.

As valuable as sermon critique groups can be for bringing in fresh air, interactive preaching at its best can involve a whole congregation. Everyone can have the opportunity of responding to the sermon. Sometimes this arrangement seems awkward in the middle of a worship service, but some have found that it works well in the seminar or forum setting that many churches have for adults while the children are in Sunday school. People can listen to the sermon and think about what the preacher said in a way they cannot when the normal service moves quickly on to other matters, such as the creed or prayers or anthem. Then people can add their comments, free to agree with the preacher, disagree, or simply tell their stories.

Often these stories prove to be the most valuable part of the sermon seminar. In their stories, people are letting each other know something about where the search for meaning can lead. For example, in response to a sermon that focused on a yearning for faith, one woman told about the experience she had when her mother was dying:

> My mother was a very religious woman who had dedicated her life to the Catholic Church. She was a convert at a young age. And when she was dying, I watched her every day losing the faith that had carried her through the better part of her life. I wasn't a particularly religious person, but I found it frightening to watch that fade away. Instead of asking for *more* faith, I think maybe we should prepare ourselves for those dark moments when we misplace our faith.

Her story provoked a response from a psychiatrist in the congregation, who went on to talk about his problems with the kind of faith that seems to imply expectation, faith that he finds to be idolatrous. "The God I whine and complain to," he said, "maybe even he doesn't know what's going to happen."[2] Such open struggle with questions of faith can do more than any preacher could do alone with a sermon to create an atmosphere in which the dubious and the skeptical will feel welcome.

Honest Inquiry

Another way of influencing the basic atmosphere of parish life is to start conversations going among the people who are most open to a discussion of their doubts and who are the most interested in an honest inquiry into the nature of their faith. Although you can find many exceptions to the rule, church members who are the least open to questioning and the least interested in change will be those in their middle years. I discovered this rule when I first offered a course I called "The Sting of Death." Most of the people who enrolled in the evening discussions were either under thirty-five or over seventy. When an elderly woman in the class heard a middle-aged vestryman berating me for the upset I had caused with the topic of bereavement, she immediately came to my defense and snapped at him, "It's about time the church got around to talking about what's on the minds of older people."

In my experience, young adults and retired people are also the most responsive to Bible study that is designed to deepen questions rather than to provide answers, but even many of them have a strong aversion to the Bible. They may have made attempts to read the Bible but given up in disgust; to them the Bible made no sense. Much of the Bible seems incomprehensible, but the stories that the average person can follow are even more off-putting. They are filled with the most improbable events: a donkey talks, a cruet of oil never runs dry, a chariot of fire takes a prophet off into the sky, a dead child is brought back to life. Before people will take advantage of the opportunity to study the Bible, someone will have to help them overcome the obstacles created by their unfortunate attempts at reading the Bible by themselves.

One way to help the skeptical get past these obstacles is to give them a new perspective, to suggest that the Bible's authors and editors were struggling with the same questions that challenge us today. In framing the questions and pointing toward possible answers, these ancient writers used a variety of literary forms—such as poetry, letters, and prophesy—but the favorite form seems to have been what today we call "historical fiction," stories loosely based on characters and events that were part of their people's common lore.[3] Once the skeptical understand that they are not dealing with a book of history or science, they can stop fighting with the "improbable" parts of the text. Then they may have an easier time in approaching the "incomprehensible" parts. They can learn to use a variety of English translations and even critical commentaries to get at the doubts and concerns of the people who wrote these strange words thousands of years ago.

One subject of the Bible that has proved to be particularly suitable for exploring doubts is found at the end of each gospel as well as in the letters of Paul: the resurrection. As noted in chapter four, any congregation dedicated to open-minded evangelism must find an approach to resurrection for doubters. A discussion leader can help a group look closely at the fifteenth chapter of 1 Corinthians, probably the oldest account of what happened to the followers of Jesus after his death, and then compare what Paul wrote with the later versions that appear in the final chapters of the gospels. When a group carefully studies each relevant text and contrasts it with the others, most of their doubts and convictions about Jesus will emerge. If the discussion leader can refrain from an attempt to harmonize the accounts or to explain the differences, the group will gradually begin to understand that their questions are more valuable than their answers and that they do not have to agree on matters of belief to be a community. That understanding of questions and of disagreement can spread throughout the congregation and beyond to people outside the church who hear about what is going on.

In time, people will begin asking for courses that deal with their questions, not just about death and resurrection, but also about matters of concern that arise in daily life. How can I be a more loving person? What should I be doing for my aged parents? How can I gain and use power responsibly? How can I be a better parent? How can I make the most satisfying life for myself as a single person? These questions, and countless other similar questions, suggest that people are looking for guidance. At a deeper level, because the questions have no absolute answers, they also imply that people are looking for meaning. As the church provides an arena for people to search for guidance and for meaning, visitors will quickly sense that they have entered a place where the atmosphere encourages questioning and searching.

Community Outreach

For most of my career, I was convinced that the church reached out to the rest of the world through the actions of individual members, whose experience in the congregation equipped them for their ministries. A physician exercises a ministry of healing. An architect's ministry centers on the design of buildings that enhance work and family and community life. Every citizen can find a ministry by participating in the political process and by supporting the efforts of organizations that serve the poor and the oppressed. Ministry happens as people bring their religious and moral convictions to bear on the way they manage their responsibilities at home, in the marketplace, and in the community.

Soon after my arrival at a new congregation, my conviction about the nature of outreach ministry received confirmation from the lay leaders of the church. I had asked them to tell me in a sentence what they thought was the purpose of the church. Knowing that whatever they said would guide our work together for years to come, they stayed with the assignment for most of a weekend and came to this conclusion: "The church is a training camp for the battles of life, and not a combat unit." In spite of the military nature of the metaphor, I still like the statement, but my growing interest in evangelism has at last convinced me that to attract certain kinds of people the church must to some extent be a combat unit, or at least make provision for organizing combat units.

People committed to social change may express a wistful sort of interest in church, but they often remain skeptical about the church's commitment to serving the poor and the oppressed and to promoting peace, justice, and a healthy environment. They can easily see the church as a self-serving institution that ignores the plight of the homeless and the hungry. Announcing that church members prove their commitment through their work and voluntary associations does little to convince the skeptical that the congregation is serious about outreach and not simply devoted to the well-being of the membership. The key issue is climate: when groups are organizing, recruiting, planning, and reporting on their latest ventures, the climate in the congregation will change. Whenever the members gather for worship, they will be reminded that both as individuals and as a congregation they have been called to serve. The leaders are responsible for the climate, but in my experience, if the leaders become interested in changing the attitude of the congregation toward outreach, they do not have to get involved in the projects themselves. Instead, they must be alert to the interests already present in the congregation and give the interested people public support.

Often the task of leadership includes connecting people with similar interests. For example, a woman whose nephew was dying of AIDS in a distant city had volunteered at a local clinic to be a buddy for a victim of the disease, a young man whose family had rejected him. When she told her pastor about her interest in forming a group in the congregation to support work among people who were HIV positive, she learned the names of two other people who had expressed a similar interest. The three of them met, organized an AIDS task force, and asked others to join them. Within a year, the task force was recruiting volunteers to work with AIDS patients and their families, and, with the blessing of the leadership in the congregation, the group was raising funds to support their denomination's efforts to ease the suffering of those afflicted by this modern plague. No one could visit the church for more than two or three Sundays without being aware of the AIDS task force. Their presence was obvious from their notices in the bulletin, their oral announcements, and their posters on the bulletin board.

Other outreach groups make their presence known by what they do around the church. When recycling bins for glass and used bulletins appear and when disposable coffee cups disappear, you can be sure that the environmentalists have organized. The visible signs of their existence in the congregation prepare the way for their announcements of activities outside of the parish, joining in a campaign to clean up the river banks or to lobby the legislature for tighter controls on refuse burning. All they needed to get started was permission from those in authority, and once they were started, any visitor to the church could tell that the church as an institution cared about the quality of the environment.

Many potential members are looking for evidence that people in the church care about the same issues that are on their minds. No church at any given moment will have members involved in every social issue of the day, but a visitor can quickly discern if the parish as a whole is demonstrating a concern for the problems that face the world. The space that the church provides in its publications and on its bulletin boards supplies some of the needed evidence, but signs of commitment that a visitor encounters at worship services may count for even more. I know of more than one person who became serious about the possibility of joining the church after being present for a sermon given by a group of high school students who had recently returned from a parish-sponsored work project in Honduras. The project has been the result of an effort sparked by one person, a veteran of the Peace Corps. His enthusiasm was enough to win the support of parents and the teenagers themselves. Then the leadership had to decide if this project was worthy of their blessing. More specifically, they had to decide if the staff coordinator of youth activities should spend time on the program and if they should grant permission to raise the money needed for the trip.

Often the most recent arrivals at the church have the most interest in outreach. They bring the interest with them, but being new, they may be a bit shy about coming forward with their concerns unless they get solid encouragement. They can receive that kind of encouragement in private conversations with the clergy and lay leaders, but public statements of support also help. An occasional sermon or newsletter article about the shortage of housing for the working poor will supply the church's endorsement for the efforts of a group rehabilitating an apartment building for transitional housing.

Clergy who have any anxiety about a loss of power in trying to adjust their style to attract people who want to think for themselves can calm themselves by recognizing how much they control the climate of the church by what they say and write. If they give their blessing to the outreach projects of the newer members, they will see the results. Or, if they are opposed to such activity, they can ignore or belittle the projects and then watch the energy dissipate and the newer people lose interest in the church.

Straight Talk About Money

In creating a church climate appropriate for a comprehensive approach to evangelism, a congregation faces one problem in promoting outreach projects: the constant need for money. Nothing can discourage skeptical visitors more thoroughly than the feeling that the church has more interest in their money than in their minds. A ceaseless succession of special offering envelopes, urgent appeals, and fundraising dinners and bake sales in addition to the annual canvass for pledges and periodic capital funds campaigns can dishearten even the most intrepid of those who check out the church as a possible place in which they might pursue their search for meaning. To maintain a welcoming climate, the leadership must exercise extreme caution in granting permission to raise money for special causes, no matter how worthy.

Even more important to the atmosphere of parish life than special fundraising is the approach the church takes to secure financial support for its own maintenance and program. If the congregation hopes to attract people who want to think for themselves, the leaders must resist pressure from denominational officials who urge them to promote tithing. No matter how they rationalize their approach, the advocates of tithing are pushing a fixed percentage, namely ten percent, as the minimum acceptable portion of household income to be contributed for the support of the church. To people who have a history of skepticism about the motives of church officials who seem bent on separating the gullible from their money, the mention of tithing suggests a particularly galling form of pressure. The justifications for tithing sound suspiciously like the biblical literalism they are determined to avoid.

Talk of tithing has become very popular among some church officials because the approach can raise more money than the church gets if people decide for themselves what to give. "If we all went on welfare and tithed, the church would double its income," declared one person who was chairing the fundraising committee. Fortunately for her congregation, everybody laughed even as they acknowledged that no doubt it was true. The unfortunate congregations are those in which nobody laughs. One colleague of mine proudly announced that by adopting the tithe as the standard for church support, his congregation had doubled its income in five years. He also seemed to be proud of the fact that in the same period membership had decreased ten percent. With the promotion of tithing, the church had rid itself of the tentative and the merely curious with the result that it could now boast a membership of fully committed people.

While substituting the euphemism "stewardship" for fundraising efforts may not have as deleterious an effect as talk of tithing, it is not much better. If the word has any connections at all for people, it is likely to conjure up men in boiled jackets who serve tea on steamships or pour wine at posh clubs. Others may have heard of stewards being in charge of horse races, but few people have had any experience of a steward who is in charge of somebody else's household or business. Even if they had a working knowledge of stewardship, the questioning people who visit a church would not be likely to make much sense out of the notion that they are simply stewards, responsible for a portion of God's estate. If they have read the New Testament, they will be further mystified; in older translations, the dishonest manager in one of Jesus's parables is called the steward. Paul wrote to the church in Corinth about being "stewards of God's mysteries," and 1 Peter urges people to be hospitable to one another "like good stewards of the manifold grace of God," but nowhere will they find any suggestion that stewardship means giving their money to the church. The congregation that wants to create an attractive climate for thoughtful outsiders will forget about stewards and talk straightforwardly about money.

Straight talk about money can follow two separate lines while contributing to a wholesome church atmosphere: how much money the church will need to carry on its work, and how much satisfaction people get from acts of generosity. In pursuing the first line, church officials must remember that anyone who has been skeptical about organized religion will want to know what happens to the money that people give the church. Open and responsible budgeting and accounting will help these people feel confident that any money they contribute will be well spent. As the leaders assure skeptical

people that the church's financial affairs are receiving proper attention, they can also help them recognize the advantages of developing a generous spirit. Once they recognize the pleasure they get
from picking up the check at lunch or from giving a little niece a ti-
ara with "real" diamonds, they may learn to appreciate the satisfaction that philanthropists experience. With sufficient coaching, they
may discover that the possibility of philanthropy does not depend so
much on the quantity of available funds as on the attitude of the individual. Individuals with a confident attitude toward life understand that giving away some of their money both expresses their
confidence and increases their confidence. When individuals in a
congregation have fun raising money for the church and enjoy being
generous with their own money, instead of being driven by pressure
or guilt, visitors will sense that they have entered a healthy place.

The Church and the Arts

People who have wanted nothing to do with organized religion
may seriously engage in the search for meaning through drama, music, dance, painting, and sculpture. Until the modern period religion and the arts were inseparable; in other parts of the world they
still are. If you look closely at the descriptions attached to the displays at the National Museum of African Art, for example, you will
discover that most of what you see there are religious objects. The
church can recover its function as a patron of the arts and in so doing create a climate that can nurture artists and attract those people
for whom art has proved to be a way of entering more deeply into
the mystery of life and death.

Most churches do something with music, but few take advantage
of the full range of possibilities that music offers. In this regard,
churches with a European heritage have much to learn from many
churches with a predominantly African background, where you are
likely to hear not only an organ and a piano but drums and hand in-
struments as well. You may hear not just one choir but two or three,
choirs that specialize in classical religious music or in spirituals or in
gospel. You get the impression that people are there not just to hear
music but to make music as a way of letting their spirits soar in their
worship of God. Churches from other traditions can never duplicate
what they hear in African American churches, but they can provide a

variety of opportunities for making music. Opportunities for children to make music in church have become increasingly significant as public schools have cut back on their music programs to conserve funds. When a church becomes known for offering music lessons and sponsoring children's choirs, neighborhood parents who claim to have no interest in religion will start showing up with their children in tow. A church with adult choral groups producing music of a quality that others can appreciate hearing will attract both those who want to sing and those who are content to listen.

Congregations that want to move cautiously in the area of drama and dance can begin by reviving old traditions. They can bring back to the church yard or parish hall the mummers plays to dramatize Bible stories and the Morris dancers to wake up the earth at Easter, inviting the players and dancers to participate in a worship service in much the same way that choirs do. Then, if they feel ready, they can introduce into the service works by contemporary choreographers and scenes from the work of modern playwrights. A scene from *The Crucible*, in which a woman of Salem urges her husband to save his life by falsely confessing to participation in witchcraft, can present a congregation a moral dilemma that makes the question of life's meaning an urgent concern.

Although the presence of dancers and players at worship does the most to produce a welcoming atmosphere for those interested in the arts, full-length productions at other times have their place in the life of the church, just as concerts do in a church with a full music program. An obviously serious play, such as *Equus*, can be a vehicle for launching an equally serious discussion, but even a lighter work, like *Camelot*, raises questions about divided loyalties and misguided hopes that an audience can probe with profit.

Encouraging painting, drawing, engraving, photography, and sculpture may not require as major an adjustment in the life of the parish as the other arts, although some rearrangement of space may be necessary. Churches can usually find ways to display the work of serious artists as well as the output of amateurs and children. For the sake of the professional artists, the organizers of art shows would do well to make distinctions among the various degrees of seriousness with which people approach creating works of art. Perhaps the best way for the church to show a concern for the artists and their art is to put the artists themselves in charge of art shows and to give them the responsibility for establishing policy. One parish's visual arts committee acknowledged the blurred distinction between arts and crafts by displaying all kinds of work done with fibers—weaving, quilting, cross-stitching, needlepoint, embroidery, appliqué, macramé—in a show called "Through the Eye of a Needle."

Once they feel accepted and respected, artists will find many ways in addition to art shows to contribute to the climate of parish life. By designing posters, banners, flyers, and stage sets, as well as liturgical items such as candlesticks and communion cups, the artists can help make the church an inviting and attractive place.

Baptisms, Weddings, and Funerals

Most churches exercise a ministry among people with no formal connection to the congregation at times of transition in their lives. Making a warm and welcoming response to these people who approach the church at critical times in their lives can help establish the climate that will enhance the congregation's reputation for openness. Some clergy and lay leaders among my acquaintance resent the demands that relatives and neighbors of members place on the church, but a positive response from the church to these people who want to get married or to have a baby baptized or to arrange a funeral for their mother can go a long way in creating the climate for a comprehensive approach to evangelism. Instead of turning these people away or grudgingly giving them what they want, the church can treat their requests with respect and in return require respectful use of the church and of its resources.

One reason that church leaders resent outsiders is that they feel used by people with no religious convictions who want an attractive place to hold a wedding, or who want to please their grandparents by having the baby baptized, or who want to stage a socially appropriate funeral. Nobody likes the feeling of being used, of having other people take advantage of a generous nature, or of being unappreciated. Even worse than the bad feelings generated is the real harm done to the cause of evangelism when the clergy and their churches are willing to be treated with disrespect by the outsiders who use their services. People who have no respect for the church after coming into contact with church officials are not likely prospects for church membership, and neither are the friends to whom they convey their attitude of disrespect, if not contempt. In my experience, the church can put into practice a simple mechanism to create an atmosphere of mutual respect. When outsiders want help with life's transitions, the church can require evidence of good faith in the two forms that secular people can most readily appreciate: time and money.

In my congregation, any couple wanting to be married must spend a minimum of six hours in consultation with the clergy to look at their family histories, to clarify their expectations of each other, and to gain an understanding of the church's attitude toward marriage as spelled out in the ritual. The clergy's time and the use of the building are available to active members of the church without charge, but the church charges outsiders for both. Couples who ask about the possibility of getting married in the church receive a packet of information explaining that the clergy do not receive any extra compensation for working with them. Part of the money they pay reimburses the church for the time the clergy spend with them instead of providing the services for which the congregation normally compensates them. The rest of the money helps to defray the costs of utilities and maintenance of the building. If the couple has investigated the costs of renting hotel space or of obtaining psychological counseling, the church fees will seem modest by comparison, but the charges are high enough to make them appreciate the value of what they are receiving. When they pay for their premarital consultations, they tend to take the sessions seriously, trying to learn as much as they can. Often they are eager for the clergy to give a homily that will pass along to the wedding guests something of what they have learned in their discussions. These homilies, combined with what the couples tell their friends of their experience in preparing for marriage, have caused many young people to think again about their rejection of organized religion.

Our congregation has taken a similar approach with people who request a funeral or a memorial service. We are willing to oblige if they will invest some of their time and money. They spend time with the clergy talking about the person who has died and about their reactions to the death. They also spend time learning what the church teaches about bereavement as they go over the language that will be used in the service. Out of these discussions some consensus will usually develop in the family about what needs to be said at the funeral, in addition to the words of the ritual. Unlike weddings for outsiders, we do not encourage the use of sermons or homilies at funerals. Nor do we encourage the use of formal eulogies. Instead, we hope that people will pick up from their conversation with the clergy the value of telling each other about the thoughts and feelings evoked by the death and that they will want time at the funeral to continue with that kind of healing process. Because we do not try to take advantage of their vulnerability in a time of grief by pressing our belief system on them, the outsiders who come to the funeral feel welcome. Because we invite them to say what they think and feel, rather than telling them what their reactions ought to be, they can participate in what may be an unfamiliar ritual and leave with their integrity intact. Helping bereaved people who have no religious affiliations maintain their integrity at a difficult time is one reason we require them to reimburse the church for the clergy's time and for using the building. The charge is based on ten percent of whatever they paid the funeral director, a system that allows people with either lavish or simple tastes to be consistent in their dealings with the religious and secular aspects of the funeral.

Baptisms for outsiders are quite another matter. In this case, the cost to the parents who want to present children for baptism is all time and no money, but the cost is the same as for members. The first consideration involving time comes up with the timing of the event. We have four baptism festivals each year; we provide no private or special baptisms except in emergencies. The second time commitment relates to the class we call "The Responsibility of Christian Parents." Everyone who has a child to be baptized attends a four-session evening class taught by volunteers and an additional session with one of the clergy. The evening sessions help the parents look at their expectations for their children and dilemmas they face in trying to bring up their children to fit the picture they have of the finished product, the perfect son or daughter. As they examine the internal conflicts that arise as they try to be responsible parents, they begin to get a feel for the life and death imagery of the baptismal ritual. At their final session with one of the clergy they go through all the symbolic language and actions of the baptismal liturgy, a session that the church urges godparents to attend. We have designed the course, including the final session, to respect the whole range of beliefs likely to be found among the parents and godparents, including no conscious religious beliefs at all. We place the emphasis on behavior, how people treat each other and how they find support for the overwhelming responsibility of being a parent.

In working out church policies for outsiders seeking services, church leaders with a concern for comprehensive evangelism will keep in mind that the practices they establish will be most effective if they do not design them to recruit new members on the spot but to create an hospitable climate. People in the midst of major transitions are not usually open to facing another major change, such as exploring the possibility of church membership. Most people need a year or eighteen months after a life-changing event, such as birth, serious illness, death, marriage, divorce, or loss of a job, before they are ready to think about joining a church, if they ever do. The objective of policies affecting outsiders should be to create a climate that lets them know they will be welcome should they choose to return. Equally important, such an atmosphere will let friends and relatives who attend these rites of passage know that they also are welcome just as they are without compromises to their intellectual integrity or to their personal beliefs.

By examining the factors that affect the atmosphere in a church, I do not mean to suggest that the leaders of the church should do something about them all before they begin serious planning for a program of comprehensive evangelism, but I do recommend that they give careful consideration to the climate of parish life to see if they can nurture the dubious and the skeptical. Once the leaders think that they have a sufficiently inclusive climate, they can turn their official attention to the subject of evangelism.

Chapter 9

Planning for Action

Ned approached the front door of the church with some misgivings. Except for the wedding of his college roommate, he had not been inside a church since the day his parents stopped forcing him to go to Sunday school when he was thirteen years old. He would not be walking up the steps to the church entrance now if he had not overheard two young women in his office talking about how much they liked the church they had found. He had made few friends during his two years in the city and he was lonely, so even though he did not consider himself a Christian, he thought he might give church a try as a place for meeting people.

The heavy doors, bound with iron straps, gave the entrance a forbidding appearance, but the notice on it encouraged him; it announced a class for "Skeptics, Doubters, and Believers." Once inside, he was a little taken aback by what he saw and heard. Instead of the solemn hush before worship that he recalled from his youth, the buzz of animated conversation filled the place. Instead of sitting or kneeling quietly in their pews, people were talking to each other. Some of the men were dressed, as he was, in coat and tie, while others were in blue jeans, but they and the women, some of whom had also arrived in casual clothes, all seemed glad to be there.

Then he became aware of the most obvious fact about the place: the church had no pews. Chairs were arranged on four sides of a square table on a platform in the center of the space. He was not sure that he would like looking at people's faces rather than the backs of their heads, which was what he expected, because the arrangement meant that people could see his face and know from his expression that he was a fraud, not a proper Christian at all. In spite of his anxiety, he accepted what he took to be a program from the hand that proffered it and found a seat near the door. As he sat leafing through the pages of the pamphlet, he was reassured to see that what was expected of the individual worshiper seemed to be clear, so perhaps he would not be so obviously out of place, after all. He also was intrigued to see that after the sermon people could question the preacher and add their own comments. Ned was still not sure what to expect from the service, but he knew whatever happened would be different from what he had experienced as a child. He was hopeful. Ned had accidently found a church that for years had been paying attention to the details that go together in creating the climate in which the congregation carries on its common life, the atmosphere that forms the impression visitors take away from their first experience of the church.

As soon as the leaders of a congregation decide that the climate is right for evangelism, they can start making the practical changes in parish life that will be necessary if people with doubts and questions are to feel more at home. To make changes that will be effective and cause a minimum of disruption, the clergy and lay leaders will need to plan carefully. As the planning for evangelism gets underway, they are likely to notice some resistance developing among themselves and other members of the congregation. Each time they encounter resistance, the elected leaders and the senior pastor need to decide if they really want to put their time and energy into evangelism.

Unless the leadership is willing to make evangelism a priority, I can guarantee that nothing much will happen. The parish leaders may be committed to ecumenical outreach efforts or to cooperation with other congregations and agencies in their denomination. Those are worthy endeavors, but the results will be enhanced ecumenism or cooperation—not the attraction of new people to the congregation. A clergy colleague of mine once complained that he thought he was doing all the right things but his congregation was not growing. When he took a careful look at where he was putting his efforts, however, he had to admit that he was spending twenty-five to thirty percent of his time each week in denominational or community work. The results were predictable. The same results are predictable for the volunteer leadership of a parish as well. Until both the clergy and the lay leaders focus their energy on making their church open to all people who are trying to make sense out of their lives, few people will come looking.

The clergy and the elected leaders, of course, do not have to do all the work themselves. If they are ready to make evangelism a priority, the time has come to establish a committee to take the initial steps. They might call this group of parishioners the Evangelism Committee, but if they sense that the word "evangelism" still has too many negative connotations among their members, I suggest that they name it the Committee on Inclusion. Even people who are opposed to what they think the church means by evangelism, including those who are against an increase in membership, do not as a rule want to talk openly about their church as an exclusive club. No matter what they choose as a label for their new committee, the church leadership should use care in appointing the members and in defining its task.

A Committee on Inclusion

In identifying members for a committee on inclusion, the clergy and lay leaders should keep in mind the symbolic as well as the functional importance of the group. That is, the committee itself should illustrate as nearly as possible the diversity of the congregation, both from an ideological and from a demographic point of view. The membership of an effective committee will represent various points along the spectrum of belief and skepticism and will include both men and women from a wide range of age groups and cultures.

Although part of its task will be to make the church hospitable to the skeptical and the dubious, the more traditional believers in the congregation will need to have representation on the committee if it is to be genuinely comprehensive in its scope. The committee will be most likely to represent a diversity in beliefs if it includes middle-aged people as well as young adults and senior citizens. In case the leaders cannot find any young adults in the congregation, they may need to draw in a few from outside the church or the committee may fail to understand the needs of the next generation. Because they tend to be more flexible in their views and open about their doubts, the best candidates may be under thirty-five and over seventy, but the committee should have some people in the middle range as well, especially if members of this age group hold most of the decision-making positions in the parish. The middle-aged segment of the congregation also will probably include the parents of children who have left the church; these parents may have a particularly useful perspective.

Another factor to consider in forming this committee is how long individuals have belonged to the congregation. The committee will need at least two people who have joined the church within the past year, because people tend to forget very quickly what it felt like to be a visitor, but it also will need long-time members. The new members tend to be more conscious of the questions that can prompt even the most dubious person to seek out a church, while long-term members are more likely to be convinced that the church holds the answers. Members who have been loyal to the church for many years also can be trusted to serve as the corporate memory and the bearers of tradition. They can tell the stories that give the congregation its sense of identity and that provide the basis for change.

Finally, the work of the committee will require that it have both men and women and be as racially and culturally diverse as the neighborhood from which the congregation draws its members. In thinking about cultural diversity, those appointing the committee might keep in mind differences in domestic arrangements in addition to traditional family units—singles living in group houses, single-parent and blended families, and gay couples. A committee made up entirely of married people could easily overlook the special needs and interests of people whose domestic status is different from theirs. Those who appoint the committee also should be aware of differences in ways of life based on countries of origin. If the church leaders are mostly of European descent, they may forget that the expectations of people born in Africa are different from those of people born in America who have African ancestors, and that Spanish-speaking people come from a variety of racial mixtures and cultures.

Having laid down these requirements, I hasten to add that the two primary qualifications for appointment to the committee should be interest in the task and competence in analysis and organization. If the leadership has to choose between diversity on the one hand and interest coupled with competence on the other, I strongly suggest that they go with the latter. I have seen too many listless and unimaginative church committees whose memberships were based totally on a concern for diversity. Leaders obsessed with the standard of diversity cajoled people into accepting assignments for tasks in which they had little interest. The lack of genuine interest in the work of a committee showed up as passive participation and missed meetings, which undermined the morale of the entire group.

The leadership of the congregation will have to realize that competent people are likely to be busy people. All too often a church puts together a topnotch group of people for a given task, but they can never find a time when they are all available to meet. The way to deal with this problem is to recruit people for a set schedule of meetings at an established location. "Are you willing to serve on the Inclusion Committee, which will meet at the church from 8:00 until 10:00 P.M. on the first Wednesday of each month for the next year, and to attend a weekend retreat May 7-9?" An affirmative response to that sort of question will not only make certain that the candidate is available but also genuinely interested, while the half-hearted may make a graceful exit.

To get the committee started, the leadership should supply the members with a statement of purpose and their initial assignments. The committee will be most productive if the members arrive at their first meeting with such a job description in hand. For example, if the purpose of the committee is to help the church be more hospitable to people without regard for their capacity to believe what religious authorities tell them, then the committee has a perspective for analyzing and recommending changes in areas that may have an impact on a visitor's experience of the church. Then their initial assignment might be to analyze the details that influence a visitor's perception of the church and to make recommendations for changes, a task that may take the new committee on inclusion at least a year.

No matter how far they have progressed in dealing with the details outlined in their job description, the committee would do well to pause at the end of the first year to assess their accomplishments, to find out which committee members are willing to sign on for another year, to replace the people who drop off, and to plan their work for the year to come. If the parish leaders and the committee agree that the committee has done all it can with the details, the committee is ready to start working on the major areas of parish life that have an impact on evangelism. If a year was not enough for the smaller items, the committee has no reason to feel discouraged. The process should not be hurried. Remember what some architects say: "God is in the details." Other architects say, "The devil is in the details." Either way, the message is clear. Pay attention to the small matters that are all too easy to overlook but which determine the nature of the institution.

The Details of Parish Life

Telephone Inquiries. What do the secretaries or volunteers say to people who call asking for information about the church? Perhaps they could be coached as to ways they might more effectively let the inquirers know that the doubtful are more than welcome. If the church has an answering machine or answering service for the hours when no one is in the parish office, what is the message? Perhaps the welcome could be made more explicit, such as, "We welcome skeptical people as well as conventional Christians to our services, which begin each Sunday at...."

Signs. Approach the church building as if for the first time. What do the signs tell you about the nature of the congregation, what goes on in the church, and who might be welcome? If the only names appearing on the signs are clergy, what does that tell you about the congregation's attitude toward religious authority? This business of signs can become technical, but it is an area in which some people have particular expertise. After its initial analysis of existing signs, the committee might want to look for an architect, designer, or advertising person with practical experience in putting up signs that work.

Entrances. Before visitors ever enter the church, they get an impression of the congregation by what they notice first as they approach the door. Are the entrances inviting or forbidding, attractive or cluttered? Are they clearly labeled so that a visitor can find without difficulty the place of worship or the offices? After attending the church for a while, members scarcely see the entrances, since active members usually come through a parish hall or office entrance. These entrances deserve the committee's attention as well, but the primary concern should be for the approach that a new person would most likely take.

Bulletins. Most churches hand out a leaflet containing the order of service to each person who comes to worship, but seldom does anyone in authority stop to wonder about what impression this little publication is likely to make on a visitor. To conserve paper and to keep down other costs of preparation and reproduction, many of these bulletins have reduced the information to such a compact form that they appear to be written in code. What stranger could possibly figure out what is meant by "Venite, p. 82"? The unintended message to visitors often is: "This bulletin is for practicing Christians. If you cannot decipher its contents, you probably don't belong here." Visitors can feel completely lost and out of place as they see other people finding parts of the service in various books. As the committee examines the bulletin from the new person's point of view, they may question the economy of the cryptic leaflet and suggest a form that tells the visitors what they need to know in order to feel included: the names of the people taking leading roles in the service (the programs at a play or football game do no less), the words the congregation is supposed to say (so that they do not have to fumble their way through the back of a hymnal or a prayer book or feel stupid because everyone else seems to know the words by heart), and clear directions for finding where coffee is served (so they will not be left wondering what happened to everybody after the service).

Communion. The invitation to the Lord's table may appear in the bulletin, or may be offered by the person presiding, or both. The committee should pay attention to the invitation and ask about the impact on the dubious or skeptical person. What is the message when the invitation is just to baptized Christians, or to baptized Christians and Quakers, or only to those who confess Jesus Christ as their Lord and Savior? Does the church think it can make a meaningful distinction between visitors based on what their parents may or may not have done about getting them baptized as infants? Does the church mean for the Lord's table to be a symbol of exclusion and rejection?

Questions about who is welcome to participate in the Lord's Supper can be touchy in places where the answers to the questions are bound up in doctrine and tradition. For many Christians, the sharing of bread and wine at the Lord's table provides an assurance for the faithful that they belong to the family of God through baptism. They will argue that those who have not been baptized do not belong to God's family, and therefore cannot participate in the family meal. To argue against the long-held view of communion as an exclusive meal for believers, those in favor of an inclusive invitation might turn to the biblical accounts of Jesus's last supper with his disciples. The gospels provide no evidence that the people with whom Jesus shared the meal had been baptized, and even if they had been, it would have been the baptism offered by John the Baptist. The gospels also go to some lengths to point out that the disciples were people of "little faith" and that they continued to have doubts about Jesus. If the last supper was to be a model for the ritual meals of Jesus's followers, then surely we can argue that the church has no right to erect barriers to the table by requiring baptism or faith. The questions about communion may prove to be difficult, but a committee responsible for evangelism has an obligation to raise the questions and to help the rest of the congregation look at the implications of their answers.

Welcome Table. Does your church have a clearly identified place where visitors can find information about the church? If not, the committee might want to recommend establishing and staffing what some churches call a welcome table. You might call it a reception or information table, but the function would be the same: to provide visitors with answers to their questions about what the church has to offer. The committee itself might want to operate the table, or they might want to recommend that the elected leaders of the church take turns being available for visitors. The table is a good place to have registration cards for visitors, cards that give them an opportunity to get on the church's regular mailing list and to indicate their particular interests. The information from these cards can be useful in arranging for a follow-up contact, such as a member of the choir calling a person who checked the box indicating an interest in singing. Or, if the card has space for a birthdate, someone in that age group might make the contact. In addition to the registration cards, the welcome table can display copies of the most recent newsletter and any printed materials that describe what goes on at the church.

Newcomers' Catalogue. Many people who have had little experience of organized religion do not know enough about church life to ask intelligent questions. If the church does not already have one, the committee might consider the possibility of creating a catalogue of the church's functions and activities. Such a document is most useful to new people if it includes the names and telephone numbers of the people to contact if they want to join an activity of if they want to get married or have a child baptized. With such specific information, the catalogue for newcomers will need constant revision as the leadership of the various groups changes, but word processors and computers have made changing bits of information a simple task. Few visitors will actually be bold enough to pick up the telephone and call a leader listed in the catalogue, but that is not the point. The point of the catalogue is to give the curious person an overview of the church's range of activities and a picture of parish life.

Coffee Hour. Most churches today provide a time for people to meet and talk informally before or after worship services, a time when those so inclined can have coffee, tea, or cold drinks. These coffee hours often work well for members of the church, who can catch up with friends they have not seen all week or transact church business, but coffee hours seldom work so well for visitors, especially if they are a bit shy. The committee will need to assess the coffee hour from the newcomer's point of view. How easily can visitors find the place? What is likely to happen if they go there? Will anyone speak to them, or will they be confronted mostly by the backs of members standing in small circles, engaged in animated conversation?

The committee can glean useful information by interviewing the church's newest members and asking them what coffee hour was like for them on their first Sunday. The committee may want to recommend that the church provide hosts and hostesses, who would be responsible for spotting people standing alone, or couples standing apart from any group, and making sure that they get introduced to other people. Or the committee may want to recommend that the leadership issue periodic reminders to the congregation that one purpose of coffee hour is to make visitors and new members feel included. The committee also may discover that they have a congregation of overachievers who are so eager to recruit new members that they scare them away. If they do, the committee may recommend that the church leaders use the periodic coaching on coffee hour protocol to suggest ways to be welcoming without being overwhelming: Ask if they'd like to receive more information about the church; don't urge them to join. Invite them to take an inquirers' class; don't pressure them to register. Chat with them about the church in a relaxed manner; don't gush.

In a way, the details of parish life that immediately determine a visitor's experience of church are easy to identify and to correct when necessary. The major areas of parish life that have an impact on the congregation's capacity for evangelism require more planning and more work: clarifying the congregation's identity, equipping the evangelists, preparing new people for joining and belonging, and finding ways to market the gospel to the dubious and skeptical.

The Congregation's Identity

After visiting all the parishes in his new diocese, a recently ordained bishop observed that the lively congregations had one thing in common: each had a clear sense of identity. Almost any member at one of the alive and growing congregations could tell visitors what sort of place they were visiting: "We are a neighborhood church, deeply involved in the issues people are facing in our part of the city." "The liturgy binds us together as a Christian community. We rejoice in the beauty and the mystery of the ancient rituals." "We represent the Reformed branch of Christianity in our area. We think that society today has much to learn from the teaching of John Calvin and the experience of his spiritual descendants who established the first European settlements in New England." "Our primary concern is for social justice at home and abroad. We understand our ministry to be in the prophetic tradition." "We are a training ground for the battles of life, and not a combat unit."

A major task for the second phase of the work laid out for the committee on inclusion, therefore, will be an assessment of the congregation's identity. How well do the members of the church understand who they are and what they are? How articulate are they in describing their church to strangers? Most of the lively churches that the new bishop visited had not gone through a formal process of identifying themselves, nor had they reduced their identity to written form. The last statement in the list, from my congregation, was the exception. We had hammered out a written statement at a weekend conference, but the exception suggests that congregations without a clear identity do not have to remain stuck in their confusion. They can get together and figure out what matters the most to them. Clarifying the identity of the congregation is not work the committee on inclusion can do by itself, but it is work that they can recommend and oversee.

The usefulness of the work done on the congregation's identity will depend on the involvement of a significant portion of the membership, especially on the people who hold positions of authority. To get maximum participation, the committee may have to arrange for a parish-wide weekend retreat or a series of congregational meetings where it can ask the members of the congregation to work their way through a series of questions:

What attracted you to the church the first time you came?

What prompted you to come back a second time?

What did you find that caused you to join the church?

What keeps you involved with the church now?

What part of the parish program matters to you so much that if it were altered radically or dropped, you probably would leave?

What changes or additions would make parish life more satisfying for you?

What would you say to a stranger who asked you to describe your church in a sentence or two?

What does the church have to offer people who are filled with doubts and questions?

The questions are addressed to individuals, but the answers are to be reported and analyzed in small groups of eight to twelve people. Some congregations have organized the groups according to the length of time that people have been members so that any significant changes in the focus of parish life will become clear. The groups report their findings to the assembly in the expectation that some patterns will emerge that can lead to a consensus. Sometimes people who have been around for thirty years are surprised to learn that what attracted them to the church—for example, a sense of community—still attracts new members although the church may now be four times its earlier size. Such surprises can show that individually held assumptions about the nature of the church are widely held perceptions, which can point the congregation to a basic component of its identity as a parish.

When the groups have listened to one another's reports, they will be ready to look for patterns that suggest what kind of people they are. They may not like what they see, but they probably will see something that a few volunteer editors can put into words. Not everyone will agree with the summary statement, but the disagreement will be a valuable part of the procedure. Perhaps people will resent the implication of the summary that their congregation is superficial in its approach to religion and that people participate primarily for social reasons. Or perhaps the summary will sound so dogmatic to some that they will feel excluded; not everyone can subscribe to a statement that assumes the church knows what is on God's mind. Or perhaps the summary will seem like an attempt to force a consensus, ignoring the tremendous diversity that showed up in the reports. Such objections as these, or any other protests, can help everyone think a little harder about the nature of their congregation. Although they may not yet agree on their corporate identity, the exercise will have raised their awareness of the issue. The exercise also may have uncovered enough dissatisfaction to release the energy required to make the changes needed if the congregation is to become a more effective base for evangelism.

The members of the congregation may like what they see in the summary of their group reports. Their parish identity was there all along and just needed to become explicit. Now that they have put into words what they have always felt about their church, they may discover that they have wide agreement among themselves and that they have something clear to tell other people about their church. That is, they have taken an important first step in becoming equipped to serve as evangelists.

Equipping the Evangelists: Adult Education

The future of any congregation depends on the competence of some—if not all—of its individual members to serve as evangelists. In every study of church growth that I have come across, the surveys show that an invitation received from a present member is the most frequently cited reason people give for visiting a church. People with questions and doubts will visit a church if they get the idea from an active member that the church might be a place where they can find intellectually respectable guidance in their search for meaning. They will get the idea that the church will respect their doubts and questions from the way church members talk to them and treat them. If the individual church members they know can talk about their religion without being dogmatic, people with questions and doubts may want to join in the conversation. Besides noticing how church members talk about their religion, curious outsiders also note how church people deal with their families, their business associates, their employees, and all the other people with whom they come into contact. If outsiders see a consistency between the words and the behavior of the church people, they are likely to take the words seriously. In other words, effective evangelism always requires both "word and example."

Whether they expect everyone or only a designated few to proclaim the good news, the leaders of a congregation have a responsibility to offer the instruction and training that members need to be competent evangelists. The committee on inclusion should suggest that the governing board assess the parish's adult education program and to recommend any needed changes. To make a fair assessment of the current program, the leadership would do well to bear in mind that effective religious education takes place at three levels: ideological, organizational, and functional.[1]

If orientation is primarily ideological, people are taught what to think about their religious heritage and how to talk about what is important in their tradition. The students are engaged at the level of the intellect. If the orientation is organizational, the purpose is to develop loyal and enthusiastic members, so inquirers are engaged at an emotional level. If the orientation is primarily functional, people are encouraged to become self-aware and discover how to find the resources they need to cope with the extremes of both joy and despair. Here learners are engaged at a personal level, what the Bible calls the level of the spirit. Far too many congregations emphasize only one of these aspects of education, with the hope—if they think about it at all—that progress will somehow be made in the other two as well.

Adult education suffers from indifference or neglect in many congregations. The inclusion committee that can find no instruction or training for adults in its parish will be obliged to make a strong recommendation to the church leaders that, if they are serious about beginning a comprehensive program of evangelism, they will have to appoint the best people they can find to begin developing adult education that can operate at all three levels. When an adult education program is in place, the parish leadership will determine how well it works at each level. Do the members of the church have an understanding of the way their congregation operates as a religious community, and can they articulate what makes belonging to the church important to them? Unless they can communicate both their interest and their reasons for being interested in the parish, they are not likely to evoke any curiosity in other people when they bring up the subject of church. Does their religion make a difference in the way they behave and experience life every day, especially in times of stress, and in the way they treat other people? If their involvement in church is merely a leisure-time activity, they are probably not going to serve as very good examples of what following Jesus can do for another person's life.

Developing or reforming adult education in a parish can seem like an overwhelming task, but it becomes manageable when those in charge break the problem down into workable pieces. The pieces in any program of education are the individual courses that will be offered. Somebody has to decide what course or courses are most needed and would be the most likely to attract students. Somebody has to find teachers and to make sure they have the resources they need. And somebody has to challenge them to operate on all three educational levels described above.

Most teachers can adapt their materials to cover the ideological, organizational, and functional requirements of religious education. Suppose those who have accepted responsibility for adult education want to concentrate on a functional concern, such as how to cope with elderly parents. They find a physician in family practice and a social worker to lead the course, but they are worried that the course might turn out to be purely psychological in orientation, with no regard for specifically religious issues, or that it might not cover the ways that a congregation can be a resource both for the elderly and for their adult offspring. What can those in charge do about their worries?

They can do more than wring their hands. Instead, they can challenge the teachers at the outset with what they expect. They can tell
the teachers that they want them to deal with specific issues that appear in the Bible. Jesus told people to follow the commandments,
which means his followers should honor their fathers and mothers,
but he also told them to leave their parents behind if they wanted to
follow him. The contradiction in Jesus's teaching seems to reflect a
pull that most people feel: they want to take care of their aged parents, but they want to concentrate their energies on their own lives
and on their children. They also may be aware of the contradiction
in their desire to respect their parents' independence at the same
time that they want to protect their parents from the dangers of
making irrational decisions about investments. The teachers know
these dilemmas have no clear-cut solutions, so they can plan discussions that will allow people to see that what they most need is not an
answer to the problem but a way to live with the problem that will
enable them to cope effectively. The students in such a class also can
discover how much encouragement they find in discussing their situation with other people in the congregation who have aged parents.
By paying attention to the spiritual issues and the potential of the
community as a source of reassurance, the teachers can make what
might have been just a good, practical psychology course into something appropriate for religious education. Those who take the
course might become examples to their neighbors of how the church
could help them to be responsible for aged parents without neglect-
ing the rest of their lives.[2]

Or suppose that the people in charge of education think that they
should concentrate on Bible study. A person who enjoys reading
commentaries and who has a fondness for arcane trivia wants to lead
a course on St. Paul's correspondence with the church in Corinth,
but those responsible for the program are afraid the course will turn
out to be an intellectual exercise that will have nothing to do with
life in the congregation or with the lives of the students. If the
course is to get beyond the purely intellectual and deal with the
emotional and spiritual aspects of the students' lives, the teacher
may need some help. Finding the teacher a partner who is more sensitive to organizational and functional concerns might be one way to
proceed. Together they might plan a discussion course based on two

kinds of questions, questions that help the students focus on the text and questions that turn their attention to their lives and to the lives of those in their spiritual community. With her particular knowledge about the Bible, the teacher can help the students fill the gaps in their information as they work with the first type of questions, while her partner might have more skill in keeping the class focused on the second type, which have no right or wrong answers.[3]

In their courses, people being equipped for evangelism should be getting practice in talking about the good news and about Jesus of Nazareth in terms that might make sense to a dubious or skeptical person. For church members with an analytical frame of mind, finding meaningful ways of presenting the central symbols of Christianity can be a rewarding experience, but for those who have never been interested in an examination of their beliefs, the exercise can be upsetting. The people who find no need to question the basic tenets of their faith may need frequent reassurance that they have a place in the community and reminders that the purpose of these exercises is to help them have constructive conversations with outsiders whose perspective is different from theirs.

Suppose, for example, that a group is studying St. Paul's Corinthian correspondence and becomes engaged in a heated discussion about what Paul meant in the first letter when he wrote:

> For I handed on to you as of first importance what I in turn had received: that Christ died for our sins in accordance with the scriptures, and that he was buried, and that he was raised on the third day in accordance with the scriptures, and that he appeared to Cephas, then to the twelve. Then he appeared to more than five hundred brothers and sisters at one time, most of whom are still alive, though some have died. Then he appeared to James, then to all the apostles. Last of all, as to one untimely born, he appeared also to me. (1 Corinthians 15:3-8)

The analytical types in the group seize on the passage, which suggests to them that Paul's experience of the risen Christ was no different from that of the first disciples. They notice that Paul does not mention an empty tomb, or angels, or a forty-day period of resurrection appearances, or an ascension into heaven. The way Paul writes about the appearances of Jesus, they could have been moments of sudden insight that validated the story of Jesus and his teaching. An unquestioning believer in the group protests that his fellow parishioners are reducing the miracle of the resurrection to a psychological phenomenon, which has no power to save anybody from anything. This might be a good moment for a teacher to intervene with the observation that beliefs about the resurrection have obviously made a difference in the lives of some people present and then to pose the question, "On what basis can you discuss the resurrection with an outsider who doesn't come to church because he or she cannot accept the resurrection as a fact of history?" By keeping the focus on the evangelical imperative rather than on personal piety, the teacher can avoid a fruitless argument over what did or did not happen two thousand years ago. Keeping the focus on evangelism also pushes all the members of the group to examine their positions. While the people who are set in their beliefs must find ways to present the resurrection without implying a necessity for believing what to some is unbelievable, the doubting and questioning students must show how their symbolic understanding of resurrection might have life-changing power for those people who currently have no use for organized religion.

Preparation for Joining and Belonging

Once the committee on inclusion is satisfied that the congregation has made a reasonable investment in equipping the present members for evangelism, the committee may turn its attention to what will happen to the people whom the evangelists recruit. The new people may need some assistance in figuring out if the church is really the place for them, and if it is, they also may need help in finding their places within the community. Some people can negotiate these two steps—deciding to join and learning how to belong—simply by attending worship services and participating in a few activities, but for most newcomers the informal approach proves to be inefficient. The church can speed up the process by offering classes designed to help recent arrivals climb each step. If the congregation currently offers courses appropriate to each step, the committee's task will be one of evaluation with recommendations for improvement. If the committee finds one or both kinds of classes missing, it will need to formulate suggestions to pass on to the parish leadership.

Designing a class to help newcomers decide if they wanted to join the church was an easy task in my congregation. We listed the questions that visitors to the church most frequently asked when they were talking with the clergy about their uneasiness in affiliating themselves with a Christian community:

Is it okay to go to church if all I really want is a place to meet people?

How can I join in the worship when I feel like such a fake just listening to other people saying the creed?

Who was Jesus? I mean, who was he really?

Is anything in the Bible actually true, or was it all made up?

What good does praying do?

I believe that when you die, you're just dead. Does that mean I can't call myself a Christian?

We arranged the questions into six topics, each of which would be allotted a two-hour session: community, worship, Bible, creeds, death, and prayer.[4] In recent years we have added a seventh session that begins with listing the remaining questions that members of the class want to ask about Christianity and the church. As a rule the questions include requests for specific information about the formalities of joining, such as making a financial pledge, and about the class related to the next step, belonging.

Originally we offered the class on a drop-in basis; people could attend whatever sessions were scheduled for topics that were of interest to them. We soon discovered, however, that one reason people took the class was to get acquainted with other people so that when they attended church services they would see people they recognized and when they went to coffee hours they would have someone to talk with. Because newcomers so frequently voiced an interest in becoming part of a community, we changed the invitation to the class, urging those who enrolled to attend all the sessions. To further enhance the community-building aspect of the course, we also altered the schedule to include a double session on a Sunday afternoon and evening with a social hour and supper in the middle. At the conclusion of this series of meetings, most people have learned enough to know either that our church is not the place for them or that they have found the people among whom they want to continue their search for meaning.

This first-step class, which we bill as an introduction to the life of the parish, operates mostly on the ideological and organizational levels. It attempts to confront whatever intellectual blocks might be keeping people away from church. We make no attempt to resolve their doubts or to give definitive answers to their most profound religious or spiritual questions. We also try to persuade them that they do not have to abandon their intellectual integrity to join the church. At the conclusion of the class, they have the opportunity to join the church officially by making a financial commitment, but many who are so inclined prefer to wait until they have taken the second-step class, which will prepare them for belonging.

In our congregation the class in preparation for belonging, which operates primarily at the functional level, demands a great deal of the students in time and money. It consists of fourteen two-hour weeknight meetings plus two weekend conferences, which last from Friday supper through Sunday lunch, at a distant retreat center. The students have to pay for their six meals and accommodations for two nights on each of the weekends, unless they are surviving on limited funds, in which case the parish will cover part of the costs. We also have discovered that if we allow couples to take the course for the price of one person, we can produce a better ratio of men to women. In our experience, men are less likely than women to think that church might be a promising place in which to pursue their search for meaning. Many men need special incentives to try out the church, especially when the church demands so much of them.

The clergy representative and the three or four volunteer teachers provide the students with an experience that in some measure parallels the experience of the disciples with Jesus. Nearly every weeknight session begins with a real-life situation containing a specific dilemma that most people will recognize as their own. For example, most of us when meeting with a new group of people will be aware of some anxiety that is caused by the conflict between wanting to fit in and wanting to be recognized as an individual with distinct views and tastes. With the guidance of the teachers, the students explore such issues to discover what feelings and pressures might account for the anxiety or the despair that they experience as well as for their decisions and behavior.

On the first weekend, the class concentrates on one situation, often a simulated confrontation with a friend—played by one of the class leaders—whose inoperable cancer has robbed life of meaning. The cancer victim, who has been an acknowledged leader in the community, expresses anger over the rotten hand that fate has dealt and guilt for having been less than honest about a desire for other people's approval. When their "friend" rejects their well-intended attempts to help, the members of the class experience a variety of reactions. Some become detached, others feel frustrated and angry, and usually a few are simply sad and quiet. Because the best they have to offer does not make any difference, they may find themselves in a position not unlike that of their dying friend—overwhelmed by fate, meaninglessness, and guilt. With the failure of their usual ploys and defenses, they are also in a position to recognize the meaning of the cross. The Roman executioner's cross, once a symbol of failure and death, became for the followers of Jesus a reminder that the failure of Jesus to win broad-based support for his religious reforms and his death as an alleged threat to the state did not negate his life. For the class members who see their lives reflected in the story of Jesus, the cross can stand as an affirmation of life that their failures and inevitable deaths cannot annul.

On the second weekend, the class might read aloud the entire Gospel according to St. Mark, and then review the contents of the story from the point of view of the disciples. When they later look back over their experience as a class, they can immediately recognize the similarities between their story and the story of the first disciples. They had begun the course because of a sense of curiosity not unlike what prompted the fishermen to walk away from their work and their families to follow Jesus. The story of the storm at sea, when the fishermen asked the carpenter to save them, reminds the class of the anxiety they felt during the stormy sessions of their first weekend. The vision of Jesus talking with Moses and Elijah, which Peter and James and John experienced when they were alone with Jesus on a mountain top, the class members can see as parallel with their experience on the Sunday morning of their first weekend when the crucifixion of Jesus took on new meaning for them. Just as the disciples had wanted to build temporary shelters so that they could prolong the moment of joyful insight, class members had been reluctant to separate from each other and to return home.

As they read about the impending death of Jesus and the apparent failure of his mission, they can identify the despair of the disciples with their own despair as the class draws to a close without their finding any of the answers that they had sought. When they come to the final chapter of Mark's gospel and discover that the story has three endings, or perhaps no ending, they realize that whatever happened next was up to the disciples. They may feel a sense of anticipation as they think about the possibility of their continuing the story of what happens when Jesus is gone. They understand both the joy and the fear shown by the women who discovered that the tomb could not contain their Lord. That is how they feel knowing that the class is nearly over and that they will soon be on their own to help form the kind of community Jesus had in mind for his followers.

Not all the people who take the class decide that they want to become members of our congregation and of our denomination. Intensive group encounter addicts and New Age religious experimenters may be disappointed to find that the Jesus story is the center of our common life, and they and others are offended by our emphasis on commitment and discipline. As one dissatisfied class member put it, "I was just getting to like this church, but then you started dragging Jesus in all the time and spoiled it." As a result of their experience in the class, other people rediscover the importance of the tradition in which they were brought up. In my opinion, one of our most successful classes was the one in which three Jewish women decided to look for a synagogue.

For those who do decide to become part of our community, the class has served as a rite of passage. They will not simply join the congregation, they will belong. They will have had an experience that unites them with every other member who has had a similar experience. Like members of a family, they will know the secret language that identifies each person as a genuine member and not a guest: they understand what their new family means by "living in the tension" or "missing the mark." They will have absorbed a certain amount of history, but more important, a point of view and an approach to life and religion that will allow them to function on a par with the members of long-standing. We persist in calling this step two opportunity a "confirmation class," partly because of the literal meaning of the word: *con* (with) + *firm* (strength). The class prepares people to stand alongside others in a particular group as they identify God as the source of their strength. The other reason we stick with the name is that in our tradition we use a ritual known as confirmation in acknowledging the individuals who have decided that they want to belong to our church.

Marketing the Gospel to the Skeptical

When the procedures for joining and belonging are firmly in place, the committee responsible for evangelism can turn its attention to what they may have originally thought was to be their purpose: letting people outside the church know what the church has to offer. If the committee has done its work well and if the parish leaders have responded energetically to the committee's recommendations, the congregation may already have noticed an increase in new people. As the members of the church have accepted their responsibility for making the presence of the church known and have become more effective in talking about what they have found at church, evangelism will have become an integral component of parish life.

Now that the real work of evangelism is going forward, the committee might want to look for ways in which the congregation can support the efforts of individuals by putting to use techniques borrowed from the field of marketing. Many church people have a strong aversion to the term "marketing" as well as to the idea that the church has anything to learn from those who know something about selling. Churches that think of themselves as liberal can turn up their collective noses at the very idea that the gospel needs to be marketed, but they should know that their conservative sisters and brothers are not nearly so shy about using techniques adapted from the world of commerce to get the attention of the uncommitted. In my mind, a congregation that refuses to use good marketing strategy has decided to abandon the field and to let the other groups dominate the public conversations about religion. Congregations need to educate themselves about the marketing of ideas.[5]

The time has come to think about flyers under windshield wipers or distinctive mailings that extend a welcome or packets hung on front door knobs that let your neighbors know that your church is a place where "the questions are more important than the answers." Such distributions can promote special events, interesting classes, and worship services. Even with the best of research into marketing techniques, the committee must be prepared to make decisions based on inadequate information. It will never know for certain what is the best use for its limited funds: scattered flyers, direct mailings, or advertising in local newspapers and magazines. It will never know which is the best use of volunteer time: scattering the flyers, knocking on doors, or making telephone surveys. As the committee makes its marketing decisions, it will increase the likelihood of parish time and money being well spent if it will pay attention to demographics and parish resources.

Of course, evangelism is not simply a matter of good marketing. Marketing techniques at best can only support the work being done by the church's individual evangelists. And the evangelists can do their work only when the congregation can make the good news known and operative in the lives of people who are trying to make some sense out of their existence.

Planning for action on the evangelism front requires constant attention to every aspect of parish life and program. Every detail counts. A congregation may not have a committee on inclusion, but if not, clergy and lay leaders committed to keeping their church open to people with enquiring minds will insist that someone monitor the impression that they are making on visitors. They will make sure that the church offers opportunities for people to pursue their questions, explore their doubts, and find ways of talking about their faith. The church leadership will never stop looking for more effective ways of letting their neighbors know that the congregation will be happy to let others in on what they have found of value in the practice of Christianity.

Chapter 10

Ongoing Evangelism

O nce the leaders of the church have put their plan of action into effect, the time may have arrived for the committee responsible for evangelism to go out of business. If the leadership has been successful, the congregation will have accepted evangelism as a way of life. Every committee and task force will by now have assumed a responsibility for evangelism in all that they undertake. Such perfect commitment to evangelism, of course, is a lovely dream rather than a likely result of any congregation's efforts in this imperfect world. Still, dreams have their place: the vision of an ideal future to help the people of Israel through troubled times was an essential element of Old Testament prophecy. Following their example, we can envision a church perfectly attuned to the cause of evangelism.

How It Will Look

The people who plan worship services in a parish dedicated to evangelism keep in mind the impact their plans will have on visitors, especially those whose doubts and questions are uppermost in their minds, as well as on church members with a long history of involvement. Worship itself, while being faithful to the congregation's particular tradition, is accessible and open to strangers. The bulletin is clear and "user friendly," and the people who hand out the leaflets are courteous and helpful. The sermons are in plain English, offering brief explanations for any technical religious language, and deal with the genuine concerns of people who are trying to make some sense out of their existence. Those who plan for worship also include elements in the liturgy, such as special prayers, that provide encouragement for the members of the church who take seriously their calling to be evangelists. The bulletins, announcements, and sermons contain regular reminders of the members' responsibility to welcome strangers in their midst, and to make known in their daily lives by what they say and do the good news they have found through the church.

The people who direct adult education are just as aware of their responsibility for evangelism as those who plan for worship. Besides keeping up the quality of the courses offered at the joining and belonging stages of involvement, they offer courses designed to attract the outsider, who may never have ventured into a worship service. They also are attentive to whatever issues are most pressing among the members of the congregation and put together classes that will help them find the spiritual resources to live more fully, including course offerings that give them access to the riches of their religious heritage, especially the Bible. As a result of their continuing study, the members of the congregation have become more articulate in their discussions of religion when the opportunity arises.

The people who have taken on responsibility for outreach are alert to the interests of newcomers and involve them in their work as quickly as possible, drawing newcomers into their planning and into their community projects. They include the newest people when they pause in their activism to reflect on what they are doing, to re-examine their volunteer work in a theological context. While they understand that their welcome of new people is an essential aspect of evangelism, they also see that their action on behalf of the poor and the oppressed and their work for peace and the environment are ways of proclaiming the good news to the world. They are always open to a religious discussion with those they try to serve, but they never assume an attitude of spiritual superiority.

People in the arts are aware of their central role as evangelists. They understand that many outsiders display an interest in music, dance, drama, sculpture, or painting long before they have any curiosity about religion. A volunteer singer in the choir is just as eager as a person on the staff to make a new soprano feel welcome. The people who design the arts programs recognize that their concerts, shows, and performances often provide a doubter's or a skeptic's first encounter with the church. While not being heavy-handed about it, neither are they shy about admitting the spiritual dimensions of what they offer.

Although no church is likely to achieve perfection in the realm of evangelism, a picture of an ideal future can serve as a beacon, guiding the congregation through difficult and confusing times. When they become bogged down in disagreements and discouraged by poor results, a vision of what they are trying to accomplish can help them make the difficult decisions that will keep them moving in the right direction.

Shared Authority and Responsibility

While every individual and group in the congregation has some responsibility for evangelism, the responsibility for moving the church in the direction of an ideal posture for evangelism ultimately rests with the elected lay leaders and the clergy, who have a continuing obligation to evaluate and support everyone in this endeavor. Sometimes clergy who want their congregations to grow in numbers think they have no choice but to take a controlling role. They see that the really big churches are dominated by powerful ministers who both attract and intimidate people, and they hear from more successful colleagues that clergy sharing authority and responsibility with the rest of the people was a fad of the seventies and eighties that is now passé. The leader of a conference designed to help clergy revitalize failing congregations announced that pastors must become "benevolent authoritarians." The assembled clergy clapped and cheered, apparently unaware of the contradiction in these two terms when they are applied to Christians. They also seemed to be unaware that thinking and questioning people are unlikely to affiliate with any institution dominated by an authoritarian leader, no matter how benevolent.

Clergy who see the possibility of increasing the membership of their congregations also may have read that if they support volunteer leaders who exercise control over the church's program, active membership probably will never exceed three hundred fifty.[1] Lyle Schaller, whose acute assessments of the church scene reach a wide audience, was even more pessimistic: "It is difficult for a pastor to be an effective enabler in a congregation with more than two hundred members."[2] In other words, a church that has organized itself as a collegial and democratic venture has limited its capacity for evangelism. Our congregation discovered that a total of three hundred fifty people in average attendance was a ceiling that we could bump up against year after year but never break through. Finally, when the inclusion of new people became important to the leadership, we had to ask ourselves if we wanted to adopt the organization of most large churches. We had observed that the senior minister of a large church usually assumes the dual role of a charismatic leader who provides inspiration and a chief executive officer who employs a professional staff to provide services and programs, a style that may work for a minister with magnetic charm if the only measure of success is growth in membership. We had to ask ourselves if giving the clergy more control over the life of the congregation would help individual parishioners be more effective evangelists in the community and in the workplace, and concluded that such control would only breed dependency.

To be faithful to what we saw as the gospel imperative, we needed to break through the barrier that seemed to be limiting the growth of our congregation. We did not want to turn away people because of the way we had organized the congregation with volunteers in charge of a variety of programs, but neither did we want to adopt the corporation style, which looked like the only alternative. Fortunately, a management consultant in the congregation showed us the way out of our dilemma. She gave us a few quick lessons on what has been happening in the business world.

Much to our surprise, we learned that many successful corporations have made a radical change in the way they do their business. They no longer organize themselves in a hierarchy of power that can be diagrammed with boxes and lines leading from the top to the bottom of the chart. To help us understand the new approach, she asked us to imagine a circle that represented the groups of people responsible for programs or products and then to picture around the circle the corporate executives and board of directors who have as their primary function supporting the people who do the work. When this type of corporation has a problem to solve or a new challenge to meet, the executives form a new working group by drawing from anywhere in the organization people with the special skills or experience they need. The new group has the authority and autonomy to take on the assignment in any way they think best, and they can call on their executives for the support they need to get the job done. For instance, when Xerox management wanted to reduce inventory costs, they put together a team made up of people from accounting, sales, distribution, and administration. The new team operating outside the old hierarchy saved the company $200 million.[3]

Although what constitutes success for a congregation, unlike a corporation, can never be measured in dollars, this description of an adaptive approach to management sounded encouragingly similar to the way Paul organized the mission of the church in the first century. He helped form a variety of independent communities, each with its own leadership. He and the other apostles advised and supported them, but they did not exercise control over them. Paul's letters to the churches in Galatia illustrate the nature of his relationship to those communities. He argues with them, cajoles them, even calls them names, such as "foolish Galatians," but he does not give them orders. The system treats all people as equals instead of placing them on a corporate ladder with some at the top and some at the bottom. Or to change the metaphor from rungs to relationships, managers with the new approach think of the company like Paul thought of the church, as communities of women and men pursuing common goals in partnership rather than working for their bosses.[4]

As our congregation belatedly attempted to catch up with management approaches in industry, the clergy gave up what little control they still had. The directors of the Christian education program and the pastoral care network no longer worked under the direction of the ordained ministers. Volunteers organizing everything from babysitting services to the activities of people in their twenties and thirties did not have to report on their work to the ordained ministers. The groups responsible for outreach and the arts had full authority to carry out their ministries within the limits of the charters our governing board, the vestry, had granted them. In the new arrangement, the clergy, church wardens, and three-member teams of vestry members accepted as their responsibility providing support and encouragement for those managing the activities and programs.

The most radical change in control took place in worship. For the past twenty years, volunteers had been planning worship services and choosing the subject matter for sermons, but the final responsibility for the production of Sunday morning liturgics remained with the clergy. The clergy not only took responsibility for the text of the Sunday morning bulletins, they also organized all the people with leadership roles in the worship services. We realized that until members of the congregation took charge, people coming to church on Sundays would remain consumers of a product—the liturgy—produced by the clergy. To give the volunteers control over the production of worship, we had to restructure the worship committee. Instead of a single chairman, the committee chose a man and a woman to serve with the antique title of "sacristans." They would direct the work of the planning task forces, which now were to produce the final copy for the Sunday bulletins and to organize all the people who were responsible for the various parts of the services. Each service was now to have a master of ceremonies—which, ironically, is a role often taken by a layman in the most authoritarian of churches. With these responsibilities, volunteers were more aware than ever of their responsibility to be both evangelists and guardians of the tradition.

Within a year of putting this new approach into place, not only had average attendance broken through the three hundred fifty ceiling, the number of pledges for financial support had passed what had seemed like another upper limit, the five hundred mark. We are convinced that churches do not need charismatic or authoritarian clergy to increase their membership. Dividing up authority and responsibility among the clergy and lay leaders will increase the possibility of attracting people who have stayed away from church because they do not trust authoritarian pastors.

Congregations that begin their efforts at evangelism with an average attendance base of fewer than two hundred people do not need to trouble themselves about what will happen when they reach three hundred fifty. They have other matters with which to concern themselves, such as how to identify appropriate ways for lay people to exercise authority in the congregation and how to equip them for leadership tasks. To be effective, the leadership training offered by the church will prepare people to assume responsibility not just in the church but in their work and in their communities. The point of training people to read and speak in public is not just to improve the quality of worship and to emphasize the spiritual authority of the laity, but to give them practice in stating their views before large groups of people. The purpose of teaching church members something about conflict management is not just to help them be more effective in chairing parish committees, but to increase their capacity for peace-making, of the sort that Jesus talked about, when hostile factions emerge at the office or in neighborhood associations. As church members gain confidence in their leadership and management abilities, they will further the cause of evangelism in two ways: they can reassure skeptical visitors to the church that in their congregation lay people do not bow to the superior authority of clergy, and, wherever they find themselves, they can demonstrate by words and actions something of value that they have found through the church.

Evangelism and Parish Dynamics

As the elected leaders and the clergy evaluate their joint oversight of the congregation, they may become more aware than ever that all the ways in which people relate to one another in the congregation have an impact on evangelism. They may even come to the conclusion that how people act may contribute more to proclaiming the good news than what people claim to believe. In other words, they may emphasize *orthopraxy* over *orthodoxy*.

Orthodoxy is a familiar word, but orthopraxy less so. *Orthos* is the Greek word for "straight" or "upright"; orthodontia has to do with straightening out teeth and orthodoxy with straightening out opinions. *Praxis* is a Greek word that appears frequently in the Bible and is variously translated action, deed, function, or practice.[5] As orthodoxy is about right beliefs, orthopraxy is about upright practices. As I study the Bible, I find it pays more attention to how people act than to what they believe. For effective evangelism, I think that the leadership of any congregation would do well to follow the Bible and keep their emphasis on behavior.

If a congregation is going to welcome people who have difficulty with believing, the members can never form a community that depends on their agreeing with one another about theology. Since their unifying principle cannot be dedication to a set of doctrines, a commitment to ways of doing things becomes essential. The more relaxed the church is about doctrine, the more careful the leaders must be in conducting the life of the congregation according to the norms and standards of their particular tradition. The leaders of a church committed to particular ways of doing things—that is, to orthopraxy—will recognize that they oversee at least two kinds of practice: the formal and the moral.

By formal practices, I mean the way the church conducts its business and its worship. The Acts of the Apostles describes the formal praxis of the first Christian community: "They devoted themselves to the apostles' teaching and fellowship, to the breaking of bread and the prayers" (Acts 2:42). Although this description of life in the Jerusalem church may represent an ideal in the mind of the person who wrote Acts rather than an accurate historical report, it can serve the church today as an ideal of what parish life can be. I think that the order may be significant. First on the list of what the followers of Jesus do appears their devotion to the teaching of the apostles, followed by fellowship and worship.

The order of priorities that the Acts of the Apostles puts forward for early Christian communities makes perfect sense for the congregation that wants to include dubious or skeptical people. People who have developed an analytical approach to life can best be served by a congregation devoted to the education of adults as well as children. Such people will show the most initial interest, and ultimately the most loyalty, if they can be engaged at the intellectual, emotional, and spiritual levels through a continuing program of Christian education. To the extent that the parish educational program includes "the apostles' teaching" as recorded in the Bible, individual members will be equipped to discuss their religious affiliation not only with their secular friends and acquaintances but also with Christians who are devoted to orthodoxy. To maintain the unity of the church, I think it is essential for Christians of "little faith" to have sufficient knowledge of the Bible and church history to carry on intelligent conversations with their sisters and brothers who think that believing is important.

Church people of any ideological persuasion who are committed to fellowship, the second item on the list of what Christians do, may worry about the impact of a successful evangelism program. The biblical word for fellowship, *koinonia,* evolved from a verb that meant to share, or to have a share. Those who are upset at the prospect of church growth reason that to possess one of two hundred shares in a congregation must be worth more than to have one share out of four hundred or seven hundred. It is true in a corporation that the more shares there are outstanding, the smaller will be the proportion of ownership represented by each share. But unlike a corporation, the church does not represent a zero-sum investment. A Christian community does not have just so much fellowship to divide, and then it is gone. It does not issue a new share of stock to each new member, devaluing the worth of each existing share. If anything, the opposite is true. Each new person contributes to the fellowship pool, increasing the possibility of shared experiences for the existing members.

People who have enjoyed the fellowship of small churches have to realize that fellowship in a larger church happens, but in a slightly different way. A large church in reality is a cluster of small churches, or fellowship circles. People who are afraid that their church is getting too large also may worry about the problems created by circles, which they can denigrate as cliques. A clique (the name is derived from the sound of a latch falling into place[6]) is an exclusive group that delights in its exclusivity. A church made up of a cluster of cliques would be an unhappy place, but as my teacher Charles F. Penniman taught, we can define a circle in two ways: as a closed, curved line or as a fixed point with radii. If we think of a church circle in terms of a closed, curved line, a clique comes immediately to mind, but if we take the alternative definition, other possibilities emerge. A circle becomes the place where people discover the fixed point from which they can move out with confidence to interact with those from other circles or from no circle. Or, as Penniman put it, people can become so well-grounded that they are free for "friendly mobility" throughout the social order.

If they value orthopraxy, practicing the way of life mandated by the gospel, members of a growing church will attach themselves to circles within the congregation. Such circles may be organized around interests, common experiences, or the conditions in which people find themselves. Many people with an interest in the arts or in outreach find that the people already engaged in such activities provide ready-made circles for them. Some find at the end of a particularly meaningful educational experience that they want to keep meeting, perhaps on a less frequent schedule, with other members of the class. In our congregation, every now and then I stumble across a men's or a women's or a couples' group that started with a single course and went on to meet for years. Other people gravitate toward a circle of people with whom they have some affinity because of a crisis in their lives: losing a job, getting divorced, coping with the death of a child, surviving cancer, turning fifty. Still others may want to spend time with people living with pressures similar to theirs. Single adults, those eager for marriage and those simply looking for companionship, may want to meet once or twice a month. In a culture that generally puts commitment to careers ahead of the promises made at a wedding, some couples want to make sure that they spend time every month with other couples who also have a stake in marriage.

In a healthy church, most members will not participate in just one circle but in two or more. The leadership then bears the responsibility for seeing that circles are available, that they interact with each other, and that they behave responsibly. If a circle degenerates into a clique, the leaders may have to call the group to account. Because most members of large or growing congregations get most of their church experience in circles, the oversight of the ongoing groups becomes a critical assignment for the leaders.

Noticing the behavior of people operating within their own circles or interacting with people from other circles will bring the leadership to the moral aspect of orthopraxy. How people treat each other will determine not only what kind of experience church will be for the members but also how effective the congregation will be in its program of comprehensive evangelism. Standards of conduct, especially those derived from the Bible, will be normative for the congregation that values fellowship.

For example, consider a typical parish conflict between groups competing for space in the church building. The Christian education people feel that their courses should have priority, especially if the group wanting space at the same time is a "peripheral" one, such as the theater company. To the directors of the education program, the drama group in the church is like hydrilla, which spreads into every stream and tributary on the river, threatening to choke off all other life. The drama people are convinced that the education people have a highly inflated sense of their importance and that they fail to understand the kind of space required for a successful dramatic production, space not only for rehearsing more than one scene at a time but also for building sets and for storing props and costumes. The relationship between the two "circles" is always tense at best, but then two of the directors of Christian education arrive one evening to set up the parish hall for a teachers' meeting only to find the place littered with lumber and canvas and tools and paint buckets. They begin shouting at a person with a paint brush in his hand, but they know that the real culprit is the producer of the new show who did not check to see if anyone else had reserved the space. They chase off the set-builders and somehow manage to hold their meeting in one corner of the hall, all the while grumbling and complaining about the arrogance and stupidity of the producer who did not have the sense to consult the space calendar before telling her stage crew that they could build sets in the parish hall that night.

If an elected leader of the congregation is present for this display of annoyance, his or her responsibility should be clear. The leader catches the directors at the end of the meeting and says, "I can see you're upset about the space conflict. The producer is in the church, let's go find her and see if we can sort this out." The directors agree, but reluctantly, because they would rather complain about the producer than complain to her. When the directors face the producer with their complaint, she is somewhat taken aback. She insists that she had been told six months previously that her group had first claims on the parish hall during "tech week," the final days before the opening of the show. The parish leader who had arranged the confrontation then points out that the hour is late and suggests that they set a time for a meeting to iron out any other scheduling conflicts and to see if they can find a better way to handle competition for space in the future.

The timely intervention of a parish leader can affirm people in their anger and help them not to sin. The word for sin here means literally "to miss the mark," that is, to avoid or to side-step the issue and the person that evoked the anger. A leader who acts quickly, who does not "allow the sun to go down" on anger, can keep groups from building up the kind of resentment that will spill over into other areas of parish life. In the process, both the drama and the education people will be practicing an approach to conflict management that may serve them well at home and where they work. Lay leaders, by drawing attention to moral principles in potentially explosive situations, do more to promote fellowship and evangelism than preachers ever can. By attending to moral aspects of orthopraxy, even if they have never heard the word, they are making sure that congregation is living up to its own standards and that the church is becoming a place where outsiders will come looking for guidance.

After "fellowship," which opens up the moral dimensions of orthopraxy, the Acts of the Apostles lists among the formal things that the followers of Jesus are devoted to "the breaking of bread and the prayers," actions we associate with worship. The conduct of public worship will always be central to the life of a congregation committed to orthopraxy. When worship is conducted conscientiously according to a particular tradition, both those of little faith and the ardent believers may come together to rehearse the symbols of the faith, to reconstitute their community, and to find refreshment for their souls. If the central symbols were to be obscured or obliterated to meet the objections of the doubters, worship would lose the capacity both to challenge and to unify a congregation whose members represent a wide range of belief and disbelief. Newcomers occasionally ask, "If the Nicene Creed causes problems for so many people, why not take it out of the service?" The answer is, "We say the creed every Sunday because it provides a quick summary of the symbols that identify us as a distinctive people. Or, as some sociologists would say, the creed is a shorthand statement of our 'organizing myth.' We recite the creeds for the same reason that we read the Bible and reenact Jesus's last supper with his disciples, because that is what people in our version of Christianity do when they get together Sunday mornings. People are not required to hold any particular opinions about these practices, they are simply invited to participate."

The breaking of bread, especially a real loaf of bread, as a form of worship offers a singular advantage to a congregation made up of both skeptical people and conventional Christians. Dividing and distributing the loaf, usually accompanied by wine, can be a meaningful experience no matter what people believe happens when these elements of worship are consecrated. Sharing the bread can provide a regular reminder of what is required for a sense of community. Unfortunately, in recent years the word "sharing" has lost much of its force because self-help, therapy, and religious groups constantly misuse it. Until the 1930s, when Moral Rearmament introduced the practice of using "share" instead of "reveal" or "relate," the verb was commonly understood to mean divide. Share has the same root as shear; they both once meant to cut apart. Sharing suggested a certain amount of loss and pain, as children quickly come to understand when parents force them to share their toys. When my little sister is playing with my toy dump truck, I cannot have it, and when the Sunday school teachers are using the parish hall, the drama group cannot build sets there. The only logical way to share an experience is to do something with another person or other people, in which case responsibility and action must be divided. The breaking of bread ritual points to the sometimes harsh reality of sharing in the older sense of the word.

Along with the breaking of bread, the prayers constitute a significant part of worship in congregations that emphasize doing over believing. People can participate in public prayer with or without any conviction that God will react to what they are saying. In congregations that permit the practice, the prayers of the people can provide the means for individuals to announce what is most on their minds: their joys and sorrows, their worries and their hopes, and their desire to keep alive the memory of those who have died. I heard someone object that when individuals are permitted to offer their own intercessions and thanksgivings, the prayers often sound more like announcements to the congregation than petitions addressed to God. My response was, "True. What could be more appropriate than people in a spiritual community telling each other what matters to them?" Although the form of the prayers has changed a bit to allow individuals a chance to speak for themselves, the function is the same as the "pastoral prayer" offered by the preacher in the church of my youth. Although the preacher addressed the prayer to God, it was the means by which we learned that Amy Sue's long-overdue baby had been born and that old Mrs. Rust was back in the hospital, this time with a broken hip. Then as now, the prayers let the community know what was happening so that people could offer one another congratulations or condolences or help.

Disenchantment and Maturity

Emphasizing right behavior over right belief can help a congregation to welcome people who were once exposed to the church but later became disenchanted with organized religion. As children they may have believed that a benevolent father in heaven would answer their prayers and would look after them if they were good; later they learned that the belief has little basis in reality. Good people can get killed when drunk drivers smash into their cars and prayers often produce no results. When they become thoroughly disillusioned, they separate themselves from the church. If current trends continue, two-thirds of the children growing up in the church will leave.[7]

Church people often think of their children's disenchantment with religion as a sign of failure. Success to them would be restoring the enchantment the young people once experienced. Conventional evangelists sometimes try to re-enchant people with things religious, but perhaps a more constructive approach would be to view disenchantment as a healthy stage of religious development. In a note I recently received thanking me for sending her son a prayer book in recognition of his graduation from high school, a member of the congregation, Robin Blair, reported that her son Macon had asked, "Mom, do you think that Jim knows I'm an atheist?" He had gone to Sunday school, served as an acolyte, and most recently had been a member of the parish's work party that had gone to assist the efforts of the church in Honduras. From one perspective we may have failed miserably with this thoughtful young man, but from another perspective we may have succeeded better than we know. At least at an appropriate age he is passing through the stage of spiritual development identified as disenchantment.

Anthropologists have found disenchantment at work in many tribal initiation rites throughout the world. Central to a rite found among the Hopi Indians is something called the "unmasking of the gods" as part of a ceremonial dance. For the first time in their lives the village children see the dancing gods enter without their masks and discover that these mysterious beings are actually their own kin, members of their own village, pretending to be gods.[8] If we compare Christian rites of passage, we might conclude that the churches have succeeded admirably with the first stage of their children's initiation into the adult world of religion. By the time they leave home, many of them have discovered the symbols of the faith to be an illusion and have become so thoroughly disenchanted with religion that they will not return. When adult Christians unmask the tooth fairy, the Easter bunny, and Santa Claus, they may unintentionally unmask Jesus of Nazareth as well, and leave their children with no intellectually acceptable alternative to atheism. The churches have not succeeded in helping the young people who leave to understand that the primary symbols of the church point to the infinite and reveal the sacred.

At the very least, members of a congregation who have found the church to be a help in their search for meaning can learn to appreciate the value of disenchantment in their lives and in the lives of the adults they are trying to reach. Instead of seeing disillusionment with religion as a problem, they can take it as a sign of developing maturity. They can congratulate the disenchanted on their good fortune and their good sense. Those who profess disillusionment are fortunate in being able to see beneath the surface of religious forms to the reality of random tragedy. They have had the good sense to reject superstition and supernaturalism. Now they may be ready to engage in the serious business of making sense out of their lives, using the myths and symbols of the church as signs along the way to guide their spiritual quest.

While a congregation is trying to figure out an appropriate way to manage disenchantment as a constructive process in evangelism, it might also pay attention to the way it prepares its children to move into and through their probable disillusionment with religion. What kind of a place is church for the children? Is the church a place where a child is considered to be a person and where the child can learn to consider other people? Is the church a place where children can find dependable care as opposed to the capricious care that they may be offered at home and elsewhere? Is the church a place where the child can afford to tell the truth and take the truth? Is the church a place where children find that disagreements can be lived with as opposed to the kind of shallow, dishonest agreements that seem to be the norm in other areas of their lives? Is the church a place where they can know responsibility because it is neither the result of coercion or of a *laissez faire* attitude? Is the church a place where the capacities of the children are enlivened and where they may be exploited for the sake of the gospel, and even like it?[9]

Children and adolescents will handle their disenchantment constructively if the adults in the church can honestly answer most of the questions in the affirmative. A congregation can make no greater contribution to the cause of evangelism than to make sure their children are prepared to look beneath the surface of religious forms and to face with honesty the reality they see.

A Spirit of Generosity

Near the beginning of the book I proposed that we redefine evangelism to mean church members letting outsiders in on what they have found of value in Christianity. I suggested that evangelism happens when members of the church are so convinced that God has enriched their lives through their participation in the life of a Christian community that they want to include other people in what they have found to be valuable. I also put forward the idea that evangelism expresses an attitude of spiritual generosity as opposed to a posture of spiritual penury. Congregations that stress what they do over what they believe can always be in a generous posture, ready to seek out and to accept people of all ages without regard for their capacity to believe. With practice, they will find that being open to the dubious and skeptical is a rewarding experience.

If it has sufficient respect for its individual members, a congregation can become the kind of community Jesus seems to have envisioned for his followers. Such a community can in some measure fulfill the prophecy from the book of Isaiah that defines both the goal and the practice of evangelism: "On this mountain the LORD of hosts will make for all peoples a feast of rich food, a feast of well-aged wines, of rich food filled with marrow, of well-aged wines strained clear." All sorts of people gather at the Lord's table that stands in their church. Some of those who hold out their hands to receive the bread and wine do so in the conviction that Jesus Christ's resurrection from the dead is a fact of history that confirms his divine nature. Others who share in the ritual meal not only wonder about the nature of Jesus but also question much of what they have heard about God. Still others do not like to think about such theological matters but participate eagerly because each time they eat the bread and drink the wine in this setting they feel less alone and less anxious.

The fewer barriers to the Lord's table that congregations erect, based on their opinion of what constitutes proper belief or unacceptable disbelief, the closer their gatherings will approach the prophetic vision of God's feast for all peoples. This gathering can be a potent symbol of your congregation's commitment to tell the world about Jesus and his message. The table to which all are invited stands as a reminder that members of the congregation have accepted a responsibility to amend their common life in order to welcome all people to God's feast.

Notes

Introduction

1. Isaac of Syria, "Directions on Spiritual Training" in *Early Fathers from the Philokalia*, trans. E. Kadloubovsky and G. E. H. Palmer (London: Faber & Faber, 1954), 95:209.

Part One

Chapter 1: The Limits of Conventional Evangelism

1. Gardiner H. Shattuck, Jr., "Should the Episcopal Church Disappear?: Reflections on the Decade of Evangelism," *Anglican Theological Review* LXXIII:2 (Spring 1991), 181. The article quotes from a resolution adopted by the diocese of Rhode Island in 1989, which was similar to an earlier resolution adopted by the General Convention of the Episcopal Church.

2. Dean Hoge, Benton Johnson, and Donald Luidens, *Vanishing Boundaries: The Religion of Mainline Protestant Baby Boomers* (Louisville: Westminster/John Knox Press, 1994), 82-84.

3. See C. Robert Harrison, "Competing Views of Evangelism in the Episcopal Church," *Anglican Theological Review* LXXV:2 (Spring 1993).

4. A. Wayne Schwab, "The Challenge of Evangelism in Today's World," in *A Notebook for the Decade of Evangelism, 1990-2000, in the Episcopal Church* (New York: Evangelism Ministries Office of the Episcopal Church Center, 1993), 9-12.

5. Wade Clark Roof, *A Generation of Seekers* (San Francisco: HarperSanFrancisco, 1993), 179.

6. Peter Steinfels, "Religious Leaders Hold a Second World Parliament," *The New York Times* (August 30, 1993), A13.

7. Garrison Keillor, "Back to Earth: Talking with a Prairie Fundamentalist," *The Wittenburg Door* (December 1984/January 1985). Reprinted in *B & R* (May/June 1985).

8. Roof, *A Generation of Seekers*, 176.

Chapter 2: A Feast for All Peoples

1. Scott Turow, *Presumed Innocent* (New York: Farrar Straus Giroux, 1987), 199-200.

Chapter 3: The Promise of an Open Approach

1. Hendrik Kraemer, *A Theology of the Laity* (London: Lutterworth Press, 1958), 127-130.

2. Shattuck, "Should the Episcopal Church Disappear?"

3. Quoted by Daniel Goldman in "Therapists See Religion as Aid, Not Illusion," *The New York Times* (September 10, 1991).

4. From "The Unchurched American," quoted in *The Spiritual Health of the Episcopal Church* (Princeton, N.J.: N.P., July 1989). The survey was conducted for the Episcopal Church Center by the Gallup Organization, Inc.

5. George W. Cornell, "Study of Faith," *The Washington Post* (February 10, 1990), G14, reporting on the work of Peter L. Benson and Carolyn H. Eklin, *Effective Christian Education: A National Study of Protestant Congregations* (Minneapolis: The Search Institute, 1990).

6. Anne B. Fisher, "What Consumers Want in the 1990s," in *Fortune* (January 29, 1990), 112.

7. Kenneth L. Woodward, "A Time to Seek," *Newsweek* (December 17, 1990), 50-56.

Chapter 4: The Costs of Evangelism

1. Gabe Strasser, "Miracles or Coincidences?"; a lesson given at St. James's Church, Potomac, Maryland on January 31, 1991.

2. Norman Maclean, *Young Men and Fire* (Chicago: University of Chicago Press, 1992), 282.

3. Cathleen Schine, "'Hopefully' Springs Eternal," *The New York Times Magazine* (June 20, 1993), 12.

4. Thomas Sheehan, *The First Coming: How the Kingdom of God Became Christianity* (New York: Vintage Books Edition, 1988), 143.

5. For an exhaustive analysis of the resurrection material in the New Testament, see Willi Marxsen, *The Resurrection of Jesus of Nazareth* (Philadelphia: Fortress Press, 1970).

6. Matthew 26:46 and Mark 14:42. At this point in the narrative Luke uses *anistemi* (Luke 22:46).

7. Frank Lyons, "The Basic Gospel Message Is Missing," *The Living Church* (June 20, 1993), 8.

8. G. B. Trudeau, "Doonesbury" (May 21, 1993).

Part Two

Chapter 5: Adjusting the Message for the Sake of the Mission

1. I am grateful to Kenneth W. Howard, whom I supervised during part of his seminary fieldwork, for giving me a copy of his honors thesis, *Jewish Christianity in the Early Church* (Alexandria: Virginia Theological Seminary, 1993). In his research Ken identified five Jewish Christian groups con-

demned as heretics by the Church Fathers, two of which were of some note: the Nazarenes and the Ebionites. The Nazarenes appear to have been orthodox in all respects except for their observance of the Jewish law, while the Ebionites rejected the notion that Christ was God and did not accept the authority of the apostle Paul and his gentile mission.

2. Hugh Dawes (vicar of St. James's, Cambridge, England) has detected the irony in the complaint of certain Christians that putting on witches' masks at Halloween encourages growth of interest in the occult. "Their own responsibility for a much more serious revival in occult nonsense, their dealing in demonology and what they claim is 'deliverance'—this, not surprisingly, they refuse to acknowledge." *Freeing the Faith: A Credible Christianity for Today* (London: SPCK, 1992), 86.

3. Bertram Colgrave and R. A. B. Mynors, *Bede's Ecclesiastical History of the English People* (Oxford: The Clarendon Press, 1969) 1:30.

4. See Ross Phares, *Bible in Pocket, Gun in Hand* (Lincoln: University of Nebraska Press, 1964), 98-101.

5. For a fuller treatment of the authority exercised by women and men in the early church, see Dennis Ronald MacDonald, *The Legend and the Apostle: The Battle for Paul in Story and Canon* (Philadelphia: Westminster Press, 1983). See also Verna J. Dozier and James R. Adams, *Sisters and Brothers: Reclaiming a Biblical Idea of Community* (Cambridge, Mass.: Cowley Publications, 1993).

Chapter 6: Offering a Gospel of Freedom and Responsibility

1. See references to "gospel" by W. F. Albright and C. F. Mann in *Matthew*, The Anchor Bible (Garden City, N.Y.: Doubleday, 1971).

2. Larry Larson, quoted by William K. Stevens, "The High Risks of Denying Rivers Their Flood Plains," *The New York Times* (July 20, 1993), C-8.

Chapter 7: What Can We Say About Jesus?

1. Charles W. F. Smith, *The Jesus of the Parables* (Philadelphia: Westminster Press, 1948), 20.

2. Kenneth E. Bailey, *Through Peasant Eyes,* published in one volume with *Poet and Peasant* (Grand Rapids: William B. Eerdmans, 1983), xi.

3. For example, W. F. Albright and C. F. Mann: "Matthew's putting Jesus' instruction to the disciples in one large group of material was most likely done out of a sense of order, and also to make reference easier for those who would be using the material for teaching." *Matthew*, The Anchor Bible, 49. Also, Caroll E. Simcox: "It is inconceivable that Jesus delivered it all at one sitting." *The First Gospel* (Greenwich: Seabury Press, 1963), 40.

4. Paul M. van Buren, *A Theology of the Jewish-Christian Reality* (San Francisco: Harper & Row, 1988), 212.

Part Three

Chapter 8: Creating a Climate for Growth

1. Thomas H. Naylor, William H. Willimon, and Magdalena R. Naylor, *The Search for Meaning* (Nashville: Abingdon Press, 1994), 208-209.

2. Quoted in William Flanders, *Who Hears Sermons Anymore? A Congregation Responds* (Washington, D.C., 1993).

3. For an excellent example of how scholars can examine a piece of Scripture as an historical novel, see Richard I. Pervo, *Profit With Delight: The Genre of the Acts of the Apostles* (Philadelphia: Fortress Press, 1987).

Chapter 9: Planning for Action

1. Category A-12, "Things It Should Help Us All To Know" (St. Louis: The Educational Center, July 1956).

2. People who are interested in developing issue-centered courses can get assistance by writing to The Educational Center, 6357 Clayton Avenue, St. Louis, Mo. 63117. They can also obtain a catalogue that includes issue-centered courses from The Alban Institute, Suite 433 North, 4550 Montgomery Ave., Bethesda, Md. 20814.

3. For a prepared Bible study course that uses both kinds of questions, see Dozier and Adams, *Sisters and Brothers*.

4. The material covered in the class can be found in my book, *So You Think You're Not Religious? A Thinking Person's Guide to the Church* (Cambridge, Mass.: Cowley Publications, 1989). For a functional approach to the book, a set of discussion guides by Anne Amy is also available from Cowley Publications.

5. See Alan Andreason and Philip Kotler, *Strategic Marketing for Nonprofit Corporations*, 4th ed. (Englewood Cliffs, N.J.: Prentice Hall, 1991).

Chapter 10: Ongoing Evangelism

1. See Arlin J. Rothauge, *Sizing up a Congregation for New Member Ministry* (New York: Education for Mission and Ministry Office in the Episcopal Church), 23-30.

2. Lyle E. Schaller, "Trade-Offs in Church Growth," *Presbyterian Survey* 75/3 (April 1985), 10.

3. Brian Dumaine, "The Bureaucracy Busters," *Fortune* (June 17, 1991), 36-50.

4. For a fuller treatment of Paul's leadership style, see Dozier and Adams, *Sisters and Brothers*.

5. Action (Luke 23:51), deed (Romans 8:13), function (Romans 12:4), and practice (Acts 19:18 and Colossians 3:9).

6. At least that is the opinion of the *Random House Dictionary of the English Language*. While agreeing that the word comes from a clicking sound,

others—including the *Oxford English Dictionary*—think it derives from the sound of clapping hands, suggesting a self-congratulatory group.

7. Roof, *A Generation of Seekers*, 154.

8. Sam Gill, "Disenchantment," in *I Become Part of It: Sacred Dimensions in Native American Life*, ed. D. M. Dooling and Paul Jordan-Smith (San Francisco: Harper Collins, 1992), 109-110.

9. These questions are based on a response to a Sunday school supervisor who wondered aloud what the church meant by teaching that a fourth grader is a full member of the church. Taken from *Preview 1955-1956* (St. Louis, Mo.: The Educational Center).

C owley Publications is a ministry of the Society of St. John the Evangelist, a religious community for men in the Episcopal Church. Emerging from the Society's tradition of prayer, theological reflection, and diversity of mission, the press is centered in the rich heritage of the Anglican Communion.

Cowley Publications seeks to provide books, audio cassettes, and other resources for the ongoing theological exploration and spiritual development of the Episcopal Church and others in the body of Christ. To this end, it is dedicated to developing a new generation of theological writers, encouraging them to produce timely, creative, and stimulating publications of excellence, and making these publications available widely, reaching both clergy and lay persons.